THE
DAVINCI
CODE

Illustrated Screenplay

THE
DA VINCI
CODE

Illustrated Screenplay

BEHIND THE SCENES OF THE
MAJOR MOTION PICTURE

AKIVA GOLDSMAN

Forewords by
DAN BROWN, RON HOWARD
and BRIAN GRAZER

Afterword by
JOHN CALLEY

BANTAM PRESS

LONDON · TORONTO · SYDNEY · AUCKLAND · JOHANNESBURG

For Rebecca, as is everything in my life —AG

TRANSWORLD PUBLISHERS
61-63 Uxbridge Road, London W5 5SA
a division of The Random House Group Ltd

RANDOM HOUSE AUSTRALIA (PTY) LTD
20 Alfred Street, Milsons Point, Sydney, New South Wales 2061, Australia

RANDOM HOUSE NEW ZEALAND LTD
18 Poland Road, Glenfield, Auckland 10, New Zealand

RANDOM HOUSE SOUTH AFRICA (PTY) LTD
Isle of Houghton, Corner of Boundary Road & Carse O'Gowrie, Houghton 2198, South Africa

Published 2006 by Bantam Press, a division of Transworld Publishers

Works of art reproduced with the kind authorization of Musée du Louvre

Book design by Timothy Shaner and Christopher Measom, www.nightanddaydesign.biz

All unit photography by Simon Mein

A catalogue record for this book is available from the British Library.
ISBN 9780593056578 (from Jan 07)
ISBN 0593056574

Printed in Germany

1 3 5 7 9 10 8 6 4 2

Papers used by Transworld Publishers are natural, recyclable products made from wood grown in sustainable
forests. The manufacturing processes conform to the environmental regulations of the country of origin.

Contents

FOREWORDS

by Dan Brown 6

by Ron Howard 11

by Brian Grazer 14

INTRODUCTION 16

by Akiva Goldsman

CAST 20

ILLUSTRATED SCREENPLAY . . . 24

AFTERWORD 206

by John Calley

ACKNOWLEDGMENTS 208

Foreword

BY DAN BROWN

For an author, having a book made into a movie is a bit like sending a child off to boarding school in a foreign land. You know your child will be changed by the experience, and all you can do is hope you recognize her upon her return. I'm happy to say that in the case of my novel *The Da Vinci Code*, this particular child has returned home very recognizable indeed . . . in fact, she has returned a bright, invigorated, and dazzling version of her old self.

The journey was a long one, though. On August 18, 2002, at 4:20 A.M., in the basement of a cabin in New Hampshire's White Mountains, I wrote the final words of this novel. In the weeks that followed, with the plot still vivid in my mind, I decided I'd amuse and possibly educate myself by trying to pen a screenplay of the book.

After all, how hard could screenwriting be?

So, it was with considerable confidence that I sat down and began to write a script for *The Da Vinci Code*. Within two weeks, I had written a hundred pages that I thought were pretty good. There was only one problem: I'd written only the opening act, and my movie was on track to be twenty hours long. So I tried again, doubling my efforts to be concise . . . slashing, burning, and deleting until I had wrestled the opening act down to a mere seventy pages (a much more watchable fifteen-hour film). After several weeks of failed attempts, I waved the white flag.

On the universal scale of humbling experiences, attempting to adapt this novel for the screen was on a par with attempting to learn golf. I'm a natural at neither, and I have since decided both are best left to the professionals.

Fortunately, as movie professionals go, precious few are as talented as Oscar-winning screenwriter Akiva Goldsman. In his first draft of the script, to my quiet shame (and great relief), Akiva accomplished in sixteen elegant pages what had taken me seventy far-less-elegant pages.

Akiva and I first met in Toronto during the very early stages of pre-production, along with a trio of movie-making legends—John Calley, Brian Grazer, and Ron Howard. As I recall, everyone was a little nervous that day. I had finally agreed to part with my baby, and they were all preparing to adapt a very complex and controversial novel. I think they were wary that I would be one of those authors who expected them to film every line of dialogue in the five-hundred-page novel, and I was worried that Hollywood would turn this art-history thriller into a ninety-minute car chase through Paris. We all quickly learned that neither was the case.

In the first few minutes of conversation, I was heartened by how completely everyone knew the novel, how deeply they were thinking about the spiritual themes, and how passionately they wanted to replicate the reading experience. I admitted that I'd already tried to write the screenplay and

ABOVE: Dan and Blythe Brown in Rosslyn Chapel.

was well aware that much of the novel would need to be trimmed to make the movie. We all heaved a mutual sigh of relief, and we were off and running.

Through the scriptwriting process, Akiva and I have become dear friends. Working with him has taught me plenty about screenwriting . . . and one lesson above all: Movies are different than books. A whole *lot* different.

I have always wondered why movie versions of novels omit certain scenes or deviate from the novel here and there. I never understood why filmmakers wouldn't follow the book *exactly*. As it turns out, there is actually a pretty good reason filmmakers don't make carbon-copy, verbatim adaptations of novels: Verbatim adaptations make lousy movies. Novels change as they adapt to the screen. They simply must.

Now, before you read this as an author's disclaimer for any differences between the book and the movie, let me assure you it's all there—the Louvre, Saint-Sulpice, Château Villette, Westminster Abbey, Rosslyn Chapel, the codes, the sacred feminine, and the quiet invitation to think about faith, religion, and history with a fresh, open-minded perspective. I want to say, however, that in whatever small ways this screenplay differs from the novel, those differences were not incorporated lightly. They are the result of two years of work by one of the world's finest filmmaking teams pursuing the truest adaptation possible of this novel, everyone striving to bring to life the characters, themes, and original pace of the reading experience.

Of all the compliments I can pay to Imagine Entertainment (and there are many), the greatest is that everyone there seems to reflect the hardworking integrity of their helmsman, Ron Howard.

For me, the most impressive thing about Ron is that his body of work, while astonishingly diverse and of remarkable quality, was created concurrently with his widely known reputation as a human being of exceptional character, kindness, and honor.

That reputation, I quickly learned, is utterly deserved.

During preproduction, I came to know Ron as an affable and excep-

Above: Dan Brown and director Ron Howard.

tionally bright storyteller. It was not until I saw him working on-set, however, that I began to appreciate his true filmmaking prowess. Writing a novel and directing a movie are as different as trying to train a dog and trying to herd a thousand cats. In movie making, it is not enough for a director simply to understand every nuance and detail of his story; he must also command entire battalions of diverse talent and keep them marching to the same rhythm. Incredibly, Ron commanded his army with a soft-spoken determination, encouraging his troops with an air of patience, insight, and compassion. The only word I ever heard Ron Howard yell on-set was "Action!" And yet his army marched in perfect rhythm. No small feat. Personally, I'd prefer to sit alone at my computer and be able to kill off any characters who give me trouble.

There is an old saying in book publishing: "The best an author can hope for from Hollywood is the opportunity to be disappointed." I'm happy to say that whoever said that was as wrong as I was in thinking I could write a screenplay. This movie has been a magical adventure and a real privilege to witness.

My wife and I live our lives by a simple mantra—to make wonderful memories every day. For us, few memories will ever be as vivid as the night we spent exploring the darkened Louvre by flashlight . . . standing alone before the *Mona Lisa*, and seeing a frightened curator flee through the Grand Gallery with a pale monk in pursuit.

I hope you enjoy the film as much as everyone enjoyed making it. ■

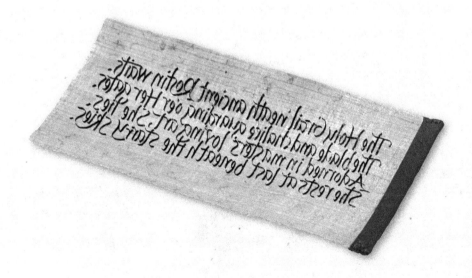

Foreword

BY RON HOWARD

Since it became known that I was going to direct a film version of Dan Brown's fascinating and remarkably successful novel *The Da Vinci Code*, I've noticed an extra measure of attention from the world at large. I can't go to a party, or stand in line for movie tickets, or even make it through most elevator rides without being asked one of the following (often pointedly loaded) questions:

1. "Will it be suspenseful and exciting?"
2. "Are you ready for the controversy?"
3. "How will you handle all the great historical stuff?"
4. "You won't screw it up . . . will you?"

My answers have remained steadfastly oblique. At first because, well, I didn't have any answers . . . and later because I was finally excited about the creative choices we had made, and I hoped audiences would experience the movie on their own terms—not mine or anyone else's. Besides, I have patience for these interrogations because when I first read the book a couple of years ago (like so many millions who have been enthralled by the story), I was not only certain it would make a terrific movie, I wanted to see it . . . tomorrow!

The prospect of making a film out of *The Da Vinci Code*—with its thought-provoking themes, tough dilemmas, and fascinating blend of characters and settings—was frankly irresistible. But the really good news was that I was not the one who was actually going to have to adapt the book into screenplay form. To tackle that job, my partner, Brian Grazer, and I had invited a fellow who is known within the film community as a wonderfully versatile and dynamic writer, working at the absolute height of his considerable powers. That person is Akiva Goldsman.

I've come to know Akiva well. He has now written (or rewritten) my last four consecutive films, starting with *A Beautiful Mind*, for which he received an Academy Award. Brian and I both know from experience that Akiva is not only inspired but also dogged in his determination to fulfill the screen potential of each narrative he undertakes.

Akiva carefully considered the offer, testing both his appetite for the challenge and my resolve as the filmmaker to put this extraordinary story on the screen. Our initial conversations focused on our individual feelings about the story, the characters, and, of course, the themes and theories put forth in the novel. I will remain elusive here as to the specifics of those inner investigations, but they served as an absolutely crucial beginning to the process of adapting the book for the screen. The upshot of these chats, thankfully, was an agreement from Akiva to write the screenplay. (Coincidentally, during the course of our conversations *The Da Vinci Code* had gone from being an extremely popular bestseller to the number-one literary blockbuster of our time.)

Before Akiva began writing, he, Brian, and I all went "under the radar" on our own version of The Da Vinci Code Tour—a phenomenon that has become a popular offshoot of the novel. It was a great few days visiting historic locations in Europe, but it was also quietly daunting. This story, upon close examination, is complex, challenging, and very much a literary achievement. The cinematic adaptation was going to be nobody's idea of a cakewalk. And no one had to remind Akiva that the primary function of the first draft was to prove that this wonderfully dense, but rather sprawling, what-if thriller could indeed be turned into a viable screenplay. Was there really a movie here beyond all of our wishful thinking?

What emerged several months later was excellent news indeed. Akiva's very first pass (or at least the first one he allowed any of us to read) already reflected two crucial virtues. First, it easily stood alongside other screenplays as a wonderfully thought-provoking mystery/thriller with strong characters. Had it been a spec script coming out of left field with zero anticipation, its quality was such that it would have initiated a bidding war in Hollywood. Second, and most important, reading the script stimulated all the major reactions that the novel did. Not only did we have a script worthy of producing, but we also felt it was worthy of representing on the screen the phenomenon that *The Da Vinci Code*, the novel, had become.

As the film's director, the buck has to stop with me, but I love to create a situation where I am like a film's editor-in-chief, plucking great ideas from everyone involved with the production and finding space for them somewhere in the film. Akiva shares that excitement for creative exploration. His final shooting script reflects his consideration of all kinds of ideas and factors, including additional research materials and even some interesting details Dan Brown had discovered after publishing *The Da Vinci Code.*

As the project evolved from draft to draft, as logistical preparations began, visual design plans took shape, and rehearsals started, every meeting yielded new insight into the richness and dimension this layered story offers.

The talented actors, led by Tom Hanks, flourished in this environment of exploration and sophisticated cinematic problem-solving. The process was familiar to some and new to others, but everyone rolled up their sleeves and challenged themselves and those around them to work hard and fulfill the potential of *The Da Vinci Code,* the motion picture. Even as we rolled cameras in the streets of Paris and London, in places like the Louvre, Temple Church, and Rosslyn Chapel, we kept examining and reexamining the scenes, and Akiva tirelessly refined his work, usually leading the creative charge toward another valuable nuance or character moment.

The draft you are about to read reflects the thousands of hours Akiva Goldsman spent in conferences with others, and then primarily alone, as he faced one of the biggest challenges of his already ambitious career.

We filmed (more or less) the script that is included in this book. It then went through the final rewrite, which is the actual editing of the film. Akiva made himself available for much consultation throughout that process as well, proving once again his remarkable passion and understanding of the story and his ability to help refine this adaptation.

My recommendation to those who hold a deep fascination with *The Da Vinci Code* is simple. Read Dan Brown's novel, then Akiva's screenplay, then see my film version (and then do all three a second time . . . and tell a friend). It is my hope that all three versions tell a pleasing, slightly different, and worthy version of the same fascinating story. ■

ABOVE: Tom Hanks and Audrey Tautou on set in Rosslyn Chapel.

Foreword

BY BRIAN GRAZER

hen Sony Pictures first asked me to produce *The Da Vinci Code* with John Calley, I was delighted. But I was also terrified. How do you take a 450-page novel that's filled with mind-bending twists and turns, and completely upends the last 2,000 years of Western history—and boil it down into a 130-minute movie without losing the magic that makes the story as meaningful as it is exciting?

This, of course, is where Akiva Goldsman came in. As I hope you will appreciate while reading it, his screenplay is no mere adaptation. It is a work of art in its own right, a concise, elegant distillation of Dan Brown's intricate and provocative novel; it captures both the book's edge-of-the-seat tension and its mind-blowing reimagining of history.

Transforming words into images is what the film business is all about. But working with Akiva to transform the words you're about to read into a movie of *The Da Vinci Code* was an extraordinary experience for all of us. The process was both daunting and inspiring, simultaneously a challenge and a privilege.

Over the last twenty or so years, I've produced a lot of movies. (I lost count somewhere north of fifty.) Fourteen of them (including this one) were directed by my best friend and business partner Ron Howard, and four of the best were written by Akiva. There's always something special about every project you work on. But of all the movies Ron, Akiva, and I have been involved in—together or separately—nothing has come close to the experience of making *The Da Vinci Code.*

For one thing, there was the scale and scope of the project. Rather than spending four months shooting on a soundstage in Los Angeles, there we were, literally in the middle of some of the most awe-inspiring art and

architecture that European civilization has produced—including West-minster Abbey, Lincoln Cathedral, Rosslyn Chapel, Château Villette, and, of course, the Louvre.

If I go on producing movies for the next twenty years (and I intend to), I am certain nothing I do will match the emotional impact of shooting in the Louvre. I recall one night in particular. We'd stopped filming because of a technical problem. It was dark and eerie and surprisingly quiet. I wandered off into a side gallery—and suddenly found myself standing face to face with the Mona Lisa. I had first seen the painting some twenty-five years earlier, experiencing it the way most people do—as a tourist in a jostling crowd. But now here I was alone in the semidarkness with this amazing icon.

I'll leave it to the art historians and philosophers to try to explain why this particular image has such power. All I can say is that standing there in front of it all by myself, my knees buckled and I nearly burst into tears.

This is not the sort of thing that happens on your typical movie set.

Then again, as I think Akiva's brilliant screenplay makes clear, *The Da Vinci Code* is not your typical movie. ■

Above: Ron Howard and Brian Grazer

Introduction

BY AKIVA GOLDSMAN

hat do you do when Ron Howard calls to ask you to adapt the biggest-selling book in history? In my case, run for the hills.

That's not entirely true. Dan Brown's marvelous novel was a big bestseller, but it was not yet quite the behemoth it was to become. And I didn't actually run anywhere. What I said was simply this: "I don't know if it's a movie."

And I didn't. I had already read *The Da Vinci Code* and, like so many millions of people before me and after, I had been captivated by its fantastic blend of history and speculative fiction. I've always been a bit of a junkie for the genre of hidden worlds behind our world, and Dan's book had certainly assumed the crown. It changed the way you saw life around you by infusing it with richly detailed and even more richly imagined history. That was the problem.

The Da Vinci Code relies heavily on backstory. And you don't get much of that in movies. Also, it's structurally what my British wife would call a feathered fish. It has the heart of a historical novel and the bones of an action/adventure. And it's full of talking. A tremendous amount of talking.

But I did love the read. And as much so, I love Ron Howard. Of all the jobs I contrive to have, there is none I cherish quite as much as my times working with Ron. He is kind, decent, deep, and profoundly story-wise—and he inspires the best in everyone he collaborates with. As a filmmaker he is a genius, all wrapped up in a nice-guy suit.

So we met in LA and talked, looked out at the mountains, and talked some more. But the truth was, as soon as he started telling me about the movie he wanted to make, I knew that if he would lead this quest, I would follow.

And follow I did. I reread and reread Dan's novel. Then I put it away and tried to write the screenplay from memory. And I discovered, much to my pleasure, that the

ABOVE: Akiva Goldsman and Ron Howard. OPPOSITE: Tom Hanks in Temple Church.

story was deeply and inherently cinematic in ways I hadn't first understood. It was a movie after all.

I finished the first draft in the summer of 2004. Ron and his partner, renowned producer Brian Grazer, had already approached their old friend and two-time collaborator Tom Hanks for the role of Robert Langdon. Now, with script firmly in hand, Tom agreed to play the part, the studio green-lit the movie, and we were off.

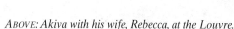

I would like to say all this happened so quickly as the result of my draft. But the truth is, by then Dan's book had become the undisputed heavyweight champion of the world, and I really think that all of us—Ron, Tom, Brian, producer John Calley, Howard Stringer, Michael Lynton, and Amy Pascal at Sony—were all simply agreeing to agree. The script showed that the story would lie down in screenplay form, and we knew we had the book. So we were jumping, as much as not, on faith.

Ron, Brian, and I had begun to gather regularly in a conference room at Imagine Entertainment where we had, seemingly a lifetime ago, pored endlessly over drafts of *A Beautiful Mind*. Brian is his own kind of savant, as graceful with the specific sounds of dialogue as he is with sweeping thematic concepts. Together, the three of us managed and worried ideas for the coming revisions of the script.

I wrote two more drafts over the course of the next several months, juggling elements from the book to see what would ultimately fit in the movie. The Kings College Library came in and went out. Temple Church fell away, sure to return later. The movie ended at the Louvre, in a train station, at Rosslyn. But mostly we were excavating, trying to see how much of the essential object that was Dan's book could be pulled up through the words and into the idea of pictures.

And then we set off for London.

Part of the fun of working with Ron is that he and I both love rehearsals. At least that's what we call them. But they're not really rehearsals at all. Sure, the scenes get up on their feet now and then. But mostly, they're screenplay workshops. We sit with the actors for six, sometimes ten hours a day, days on end, all together, sometimes in smaller groups, and we run the scenes. We listen to them. We talk about them. We improvise. And then, at night, or at the end of a few days, I rewrite them. And we go at it again.

There is no one secret to good filmmaking. But if there is a leg up, I am convinced it is this process. It is certainly not for the faint of heart, nor is it for the insecure or the tyrannical. You go into the room knowing everything is up for grabs. Best idea wins. But if you have the supreme good luck of working with a confident and visionary director like Ron, and a brilliant actor like Hanks, not to mention

ABOVE: Akiva with his wife, Rebecca, at the Louvre.

the extraordinary Ian McKellen, Audrey Tautou, Jean Reno, Paul Bettany, and Alfred Molina, you can work your script until you have created an object that is a true collaborative expression of the filmmakers, before you ever get to set.

We worked the script that way for two weeks in May and again for another two weeks in June, all in London. It was during the second of these periods that Dan first became involved. No easy task for authors in general, this transformation and distillation of their work into screenplay form. Even less so, I am sure, if you've written the bestselling book of all time. Screenwriters and the novelists whom they adapt are not the most natural of bedfellows.

Dan had notes, I had responses. But slowly it became clear that we liked talking, asked similar questions, and, of course, were now both immersed in the exact same narrative world. And I think, for two fellows who are used to occupying our imagined worlds alone, it became kind of fun.

So Dan went from mysterious author to frequent visitor and constant friend of the filmmaking process. I can't count the number of times one of us would turn to another and say, "Ask Dan." "Call Dan." "Where's Dan?"

And what a filmmaking process it was. We spent half the year in Europe. At the heart of the experience was a filmmaking collaborative that Brian has called "the partnership": director leading producer, actor, and (as unlikely as it might seem in a Hollywood production) writer, all working together. Ron believes in the writer's participation during shooting in a way that is both rare and precious. And we continued to evolve the script as we shot, letting, as the old saying goes, the movie teach us how to make the movie.

What follows is not that first script I wrote. Nor is it a reflection of the movie as it exists today. Unlike many "shooting scripts," it has not been adjusted to accommodate the final cut of the film. It contains dialogue, structural choices, even entire scenes that are not in the movie. This script reflects the written version of the scenes on the day we shot them. As such, it is its own unique version of *The Da Vinci Code*. Not as detailed or rich as Dan's novel. Not as sleek or crucial as Ron's movie.

It's a feathered fish of its own. ▪

ABOVE: Audrey Tautou, Akiva Goldsman, and Tom Hanks.

Robert Langdon
TOM HANKS

Sophie Neveu
AUDREY TAUTOU

Captain
Bezu Fache
JEAN RENO

Cast

Sir Leigh Teabing
IAN MCKELLEN

Bishop Manuel
Aringarosa
ALFRED MOLINA

Illustrations by costume designer Daniel Orlandi.
All photos by Albert Watson unless noted.

Lt. Jerome Collet
ETIENNE CHICOT

Remy Legaludec
JEAN-YVES BERTELOOT

Jacques Sauniere
JEAN-PIERRE MARIELLE

Silas
PAUL BETTANY

THE

DaVinci

CODE

Illustrated Screenplay

INT. LOUVRE MUSEUM – GRANDE GALERIE – NIGHT
EYES painted by masters stare down from the walls of this cavernous room. (OVER) SOUNDS approach, unfamiliar here. GRUNTING, desperate, SCRAMBLING feet on marble floors.

A MAN races in through the gallery's vaulted archway, moving too fast, heart beating too hard for his 70-year-old frame. This is JACQUES SAUNIERE and he is running for his life.

FADE IN ON:

EXT. FRENCH COUNTRYSIDE – DAY
An old STONE FARMHOUSE sits atop the crest of a grass-covered hill, lights in the windows, smoke a kite from the chimney.

JUMP CLOSER

Appearances can deceive. All is not peaceful here. SOUNDS of struggle within. A man's angry VOICE, then a GIRL's.

JUMP CLOSER

The heavy wooden door swings open. A GIRL, maybe 14, pushes out, lovely face streaked with tears.

She stumbles a few steps, turns back to this house, eyes filled with anger, betrayal, as a shadow fills the doorway.

JUMP CLOSER

HOLD on her eyes.

TITLE SEQUENCE

24   *Note: **BOLD-FACED** dialogue in this screenplay is spoken in French with English subtitles in the film.*

Sauniere grabs the painting nearest him, a sweeping Caravaggio, and with all his might, heaves it off the wall onto the floor.

A GIANT METAL GATE comes SLAMMING down at the gallery's arched entrance, turning this room into the most gilded of cages.

VOICE *(over)*
Stop now. Do not move.

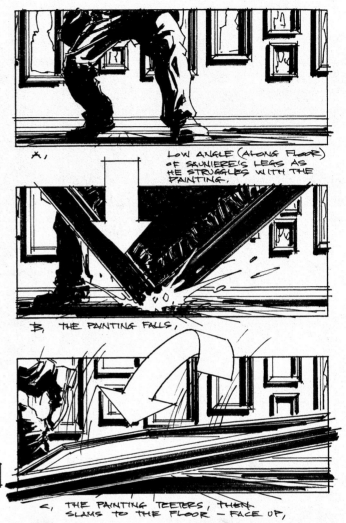

A. LOW ANGLE (ALONG FLOOR) OF SAUNIERE'S LEGS AS HE STRUGGLES WITH THE PAINTING.

B. THE PAINTING FALLS.

C. THE PAINTING TEETERS, THEN SLAMS TO THE FLOOR — FACE UP.

(LOW ANGLE) JACQUES SAUNIÈRE RUNS PAST/OVER CAMERA.

A. HIGH ANGLE (LOOKING STRAIGHT DOWN), CAMERA ON CRANE TRACKS SAUNIERE, A MENACING SHADOW FOLLOWS HIM.

TRACKING CRANE

B. CAMERA TRACKS SAUNIERE AS HE VEERS AND GRABS A PAINTING. GALLERY ALARMS GO OFF.

TRACKING CRANE

The Storyboard Tells the Story

Storyboards are a way of visualizing scenes and sequences in two dimensions, before rendering them on film. Storyboards can also provide inspiration for the visual tone of a sequence. For *The Da Vinci Code*, often two or three storyboard artists rendered their versions of the same sequence—in order to give Ron Howard different perspectives on the same scripted material.

Storyboards by Robert Ballantyne.

Sauniere looks up. Maybe ten feet away, on the other side of the gate, another MAN faces him. More striking than his monk's robes is his shock-white hair, ghost's skin, pale albino's eyes. This is SILAS. And in his hand he holds a gun.

SILAS
Tell me where it is.

D, CAMERA WHIP-PANS TO ENTRYWAY AS A METAL GATE COMES DOWN.

SILAS STEPS FORWARD, MASKED BY SHADOW.

A, THE GATE SLAMS DOWN.

B, SILAS STEPS INTO FRAME, SAUNIERE BACKS AWAY.

A,
VOICE
"STOP NOW."

26

SAUNIERE

Please. I don't —

SILAS

You and your brethren possess what is not rightfully yours.

SAUNIERE

I don't know what you're talking about.

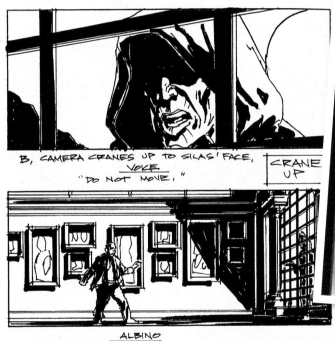

B, CAMERA CRANES UP TO SILAS' FACE,
VO/CE
"DO NOT MOVE,"

CRANE
UP

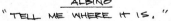

ALBINO
"TELL ME WHERE IT IS,"

The albino trains his gun on Sauniere.

SILAS

Is it a secret you will die for?

Sauniere lowers his head, has begun to WHIMPER.

SAUNIERE

Please.

SAUNIERE :
"PLEASE, I DON'T --"

Storyboards by Robert Ballantyne.

27

SILAS
Very well.

The albino CLICKS back the hammer with his thumb.

SAUNIERE
Wait.

The old man's eyes go up. Wet with fear.

SAUNIERE
Dear God, forgive me.

EXT. LOUVRE MUSEUM – NIGHT
Through the skylight ceiling, we see Sauniere TALKING, head shaking in despair, saying words we cannot hear.

The albino listens patiently and when he is satisfied, aims his gun towards the old man's sudden, silent screams.

A muzzle's FLASH.

MAN (over)
Check. Check. Can you hear me?

INT. AMERICAN UNIVERSITY OF PARIS – NIGHT
A MAN stands over a cherry-wood lectern, attaching a lapel mic to his shirt. Keenly intelligent eyes that belie a slight smile. This is PROFESSOR ROBERT LANGDON.

> **LANGDON**
> Okay, you can hear me.

AFFIRMATIONS from the packed lecture hall before him.

> **LANGDON**
> Symbols are a language that can tell us about our past.

Langdon reaches for a projector control on the lectern.

> **LANGDON**
> As the saying goes, a picture can speak a thousand words.

He activates the projector.

> **LANGDON**
> But which words?

Images flash behind him.

> **LANGDON**
> Interpret this symbol. First thing comes to mind. Go.

A white pointed hat, its sinister lines familiar.

STUDENT #1
Hatred. Racism.

STUDENT #2
Ku Klux Klan.

The image widens, not Klan robes but white priests' garb.

LANGDON
They'd disagree with you in Spain.
There, they're priests' robes.

Next is a thick-fingered hand around a pitchfork.

LANGDON
Now this? Fast.

STUDENT #3
Evil.

STUDENT #4
La fourche du Diable.

STUDENT #3
(translating)
Devil's pitchfork.

Widen to show the wielder is a kindly old man with a flowing beard seated below the ocean, smiling out bubbles.

LANGDON
Poor old Poseidon. That's his trident.
Symbol of power for millions of ancients. Now this.

Now Madonna and Child.

STUDENT #4
Madonna and Child.

STUDENT #1
Faith. Christianity.

Now widen to show its date: 10,000 BC.

The Power of Symbols

In order to localize Langdon's expertise in symbols, a new scene (not present in the book) was created. This scene tries to echo the various Langdon flashbacks found in the novel. Here, a lecture on symbology is built around powerful symbols

out of history. It should be noted that the photograph, sculpture, and painting pictured here were all specifically created for the movie. All three images, however, are real and appear frequently in history.

LANGDON

Or the pagan god Horus and his mother, Isis, centuries before Christ's birth.

The projector continues to flash images, ever faster.

LANGDON

How we view our past determines *actively* our ability to understand the present.

Mic STATICS. Langdon unclips it, steps forward, in front of the podium, now using only his VOICE.

LANGDON

So, how do we sift truth from belief? How do we penetrate years of historical distortion to find original truth? How do we write our own histories, personally or culturally, and thereby define ourselves? That will be our discussion tonight.

INT. AMERICAN UNIVERSITY OF PARIS – RECEPTION HALL – LATER

Wooden doors swing open as a MAN in a trenchcoat rushes in, puffing a cigar. FAVOR him as he heads up the steps towards a HUMMING cocktail reception already in progress.

The fellow moves somewhat uncomfortably through the erudite gathering, locates the densest group not far ahead.

Langdon is at the center of the small crowd, signing copies of his new book: *Symbols of the Sacred Feminine.*

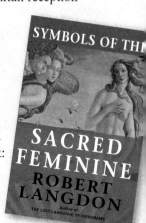

COLLET
Would you take a look at this photo please?

He hands Langdon a Polaroid. Langdon goes still.

COLLET
My captain had hoped, considering
your expertise, and the markings on
the body, you might assist us.

Collet lifts Langdon's jacket off the chair.

AMERICAN WOMAN
My son is a student of yours at
Harvard. Michael Culp? He adores
you. He says you're the best teacher
he's ever had.

Langdon's signing her book, smiles now, self-effacing.

**INT. AMERICAN UNIVERSITY OF PARIS – WALKING
– MOMENTS LATER**
Langdon and Collet cross the room towards the doors.

COLLET
It was taken less than an hour ago.
Inside the Louvre.

LANGDON
Ah, yes. Ms. Culp, I gave Michael an
A-minus already, didn't I?

She LAUGHS, maybe flirting a little.

LANGDON
I was supposed to have a drink with
him earlier tonight.

COLLET
Yes. We know.

MAN
Mr. Langdon?

Langdon looks up, patient.

MAN
Professor. I am Lieutenant
Collet. Direction Centrale
Police Judiciaire.

This small, walking cloud of cigar smoke
gets his attention. Several paces off, a
uniformed COP waits.

*ABOVE: Associate producer Louisa Velis
(right) and Cheryl Howard (left), who has a
good-luck cameo in each of the director's films.*

The briefest of beats.

> COLLET
>
> We found your name in his daily planner.
> Was he in good health?

> LANGDON
>
> I'm sorry?

> COLLET
>
> When you had these drinks together?

> LANGDON
>
> He never showed up. I waited over
> an hour.

Collet nods. Langdon is fixed on the photo in his hand.

> LANGDON
>
> Why would someone do this to him?

> COLLET
>
> Ah. You misunderstand, Professor. He
> was shot, yes.

Collet takes back the picture, slips it in his jacket.

> COLLET
>
> But what you see in the photograph,
> Monsieur Sauniere did to himself.

**EXT. BROWNSTONE – RUE LA BRUYERE – PARIS
– NIGHT**

Spindly elms rock their shadows on the ample brownstone. A light goes on in a window on the second floor.

**INT. BROWNSTONE – BEDROOM – RUE LA BRUYERE
– PARIS**

Spartan. Hardwood floors, pine dresser, a wool blanket in the corner on the floor. Silas is on a cell phone. WORDS exchanged are LATIN.

> SILAS
>
> Teacher. All are gone. The *sénéchaux*
> and the Grand Master himself.

The VOICE on the other end of the line responds in WHISPERS.

> TEACHER
>
> Then I assume you have the location.

> SILAS
>
> Confirmed by all. Independently.

> TEACHER
>
> I had feared the brotherhood's penchant for secrecy might prevail.

> SILAS
>
> The prospect of death is strong motivation.

On the other end of the line is a humorless LAUGH.

> SILAS
>
> It is here. In Paris. It hides beneath the
> rose in Saint-Sulpice.

> TEACHER
>
> Inside a house of the Lord. How they
> mock us.

> SILAS
>
> As they have for centuries.

> TEACHER
>
> You have done a great service to God.

We have waited hundreds of years for this. You will go forth.

As the line DISCONNECTS, Silas stands and disrobes. Pale skin, never kissed by sun. His back is a brutal history of violence in scarred flesh. He kneels, naked.

From his thigh, he removes a spiked leather cilice belt of metal barbs, revealing bloody holes and scars there.

He moves the belt to a similar scar pad on his other leg. Grabbing the buckle, he cinches the belt one notch tighter.

Silas lifts a knotted rope from the floor, begins to flagellate himself. His face goes back in agony.

SILAS
Castigo corpus meum.

EXT. LOUVRE – PARIS – NIGHT – ESTABLISHING
A police car approaches the giant glass pyramid that heralds the entrance to the Louvre.

EXT. LOUVRE – MAIN ENTRANCE – NIGHT
Langdon emerges from the car. Collet looks out his window.

COLLET
The captain is expecting you.

Before Langdon can respond, the uniform is already driving off. Langdon stares after.

LANGDON
Okay.

Langdon looks up, taking in the mighty glass pyramid. A man rises on the platform elevator, comes to the doors. Black eyes and demeanor have earned his nickname: the Bull.

FACHE
Mr. Langdon?

LANGDON
Yes. Hello.

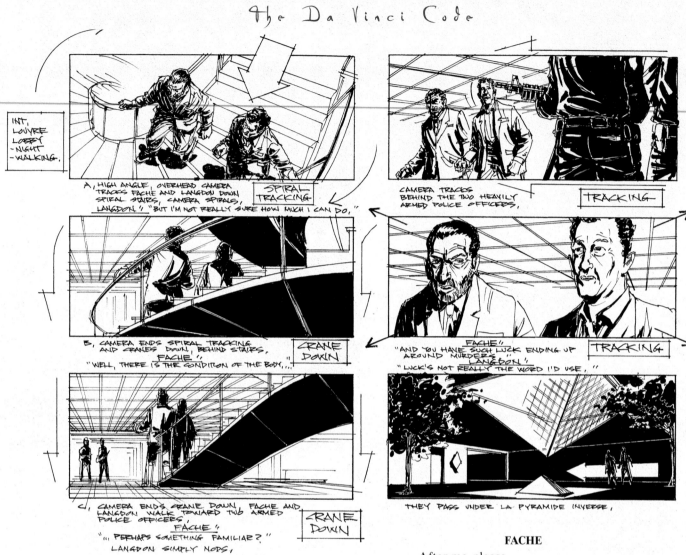

INT. LOUVRE LOBBY - NIGHT - WALKING.

A, HIGH ANGLE, OVERHEAD CAMERA TRACKS FACHE AND LANGDON DOWN SPIRAL STAIRS, CAMERA SPIRALS,
LANGDON: "BUT I'M NOT REALLY SURE HOW MUCH I CAN DO,"

SPIRAL TRACKING

CAMERA TRACKS BEHIND THE TWO HEAVILY ARMED POLICE OFFICERS,

TRACKING

B, CAMERA ENDS SPIRAL TRACKING AND CRANES DOWN, BEHIND STAIRS,
FACHE: "WELL, THERE IS THE CONDITION OF THE BODY,..."

CRANE DOWN

FACHE: "AND YOU HAVE SUCH LUCK ENDING UP AROUND MURDERS,"
LANGDON: "LUCK'S NOT REALLY THE WORD I'D USE,"

TRACKING

C, CAMERA ENDS CRANE DOWN, FACHE AND LANGDON WALK TOWARD TWO ARMED POLICE OFFICERS,
FACHE: "... PERHAPS SOMETHING FAMILIAR?"
LANGDON SIMPLY NODS,

CRANE DOWN

THEY PASS UNDER LA PYRAMIDE INVERSE,

FACHE
After me, please.

FACHE
I am Captain Bezu Fache. You like our pyramid?

LANGDON
Magnificent.

FACHE
A scar on the face of Paris.

Langdon winces. Fache has pushed open the glass door, is already heading back inside.

INT. LOUVRE MUSEUM – STAIRS – NIGHT – HIGH ANGLE
The pair descend the curving steps into the barren, 70,000-square-foot grotto.

LANGDON
The pairing of these two pyramids is unique.

INT. LOUVRE MUSEUM – LOBBY – NIGHT – WALKING
As Langdon and Fache pass La Pyramide Inversée, Langdon makes a V with his palms, fingers touching fingers.

Storyboards by Robert Ballantyne.

LANGDON
The two are geometric echoes.

Langdon inverts the shape, gesturing across the floor to the smaller, upright pyramid.

LANGDON
The anti-structure is a perfect partner to the larger.

FACHE
Fascinating.

A, THEY WALK BEHIND THE GLASS PYRAMID,
LANGDON "
"YOU KNOW THESE TWO HAVE THE
EXACT SAME PROPORTIONS?"

B, CAMERA DOLLIES BEHIND GLASS AND
PIVOTS TO FOLLOW THEM,
LANGDON "
"WHEN I.M PEI DESIGNED THE ONE OVERHEAD,"

DOLLY AND PIVOT

MATCHING C.U, DOLLY AND PIVOT,
LANGDON "
",,, HE CREATED THIS LITTLE ONE AS
ITS PERFECT OPPOSITE,"

MATCHING DOLLY & PIVOT

By Fache's expression, really anything but.

LANGDON
I'm not sure how much help I'm going to be here this evening.

INT. LOUVRE MUSEUM – DENON WING – WALKING – CONTINUOUS

FACHE
How well did you know the curator?

LANGDON
Not at all. We only met once. We were on a panel together.

Langdon's sudden smile is wistful.

FACHE
Something is funny?

LANGDON
We didn't agree on much. Frankly, I was surprised when he contacted me.

THEY WALK AWAY FROM THE PYRAMIDS, LANGDON
PAUSES TO LOOK BACK,

CLOSER - LANGDON IS FRAMED BETWEEN THE
"BLADE" AND THE "CHALICE" -- WHICH RESEMBLE
SHARP TEETH,

They have come to an elevator. Fache rings the call button, ENTERS through opening doors. Langdon stops, stares inside.

> **LANGDON**
> Can we take the stairs?

INT. LOUVRE MUSEUM – ELEVATOR – ASCENDING – CONTINUOUS
Langdon fixes on details. Floor buttons. Lights. On Fache's lapel, a simple cross called *The Cross in the World*.

> **FACHE**
> So *Sauniere* requested tonight's meeting?

> **LANGDON**
> Yes.

> **FACHE**
> When?

> **LANGDON**
> Today.

> **FACHE**
> How? Did he call you?

> **LANGDON**
> E-mail. He heard I was in Paris. Had something to discuss.

> **FACHE**
> What?

Langdon shrugs, wipes small, forming beads of sweat off his forehead.

> **FACHE**
> You seem . . . uncomfortable.

Langdon continues staring down. Fache simply nods. Elevator doors finally open.

Filming at the Louvre

ll exteriors were shot on location at the Louvre—just the cast and crew in the middle of Paris at night. The interiors were mostly filmed at Pinewood Studios on the 007 Stage, the largest in England, where there was more flexibility with shooting hours and fewer restrictions on lighting the Louvre's precious artwork. Production designer Allan Cameron and his team built a four-hundred-foot section of the famous Grand Gallery in perfect replica—down to individual columns and patterns in the parquet floor. One hundred and twenty paintings were replicated, including six copies of *Madonna of the Rocks* and three Caravaggios (whose frames were built in different weights—including light rubber so Jean-

Pierre Marielle (Sauniere) could easily pull the enormous painting off the wall). All artwork was photographed digitally and then painted by real artists, who used crackling techniques and glazes to give authenticity to the reproductions of these masterpieces.

Above: (left to right) Candide Franklyn (Steadicam Operator), Bill Connor (1st Assistant Director), Ron Howard, Salvatore Totino (Director of Photography), Akiva Goldsman (seated), Annie Penn (Script Supervisor), John Flemming (Key Grip).

INT. LOUVRE MUSEUM – RED GALLERY – CONTINUOUS

Fache and Langdon cross the vast space under the high ceilings of the Louvre Red Gallery.

> **LANGDON**
> Any of those real?

Breathing again, Langdon clocks the hanging security cameras.

> **FACHE**
> Of course not.

Fache seems almost interested.

> **FACHE**
> So you know something of security procedures?

(OVER) VOICES echo down the corridor. Passing, Langdon can see into a curator's small OFFICE, POLICE inside.

> **LANGDON**
> I know video surveillance in a museum this size is cost-prohibitive. Most now rely on containment.

> **FACHE**
> Yes. Forget about keeping the criminals out. Now we keep them in.

INT. LOUVRE – SALON CARRE – WALKING – CONTINUOUS

Ahead is the arched entrance to the Grande Galerie. The security gate has been partially raised.

> **LANGDON**
> Ah, the Grande Galerie. This is where you found the body.

> **FACHE**
> How would you know that?

> **LANGDON**
> I recognized the parquet floors in the Polaroid. They're unmistakable.

From this angle, Langdon can see the felled canvas.

> **LANGDON**
> My God. That's a Caravaggio.

> **FACHE**
> We believe the curator was attacked in the rear gallery.

> **LANGDON**
> He fled here and pulled the painting off the wall.

Langdon watches a ghostly Sauniere run past him, pursued by a figure who is only an indistinct blur.

Storyboards by Robert Ballantyne.

LANGDON
He activated the security gate to trap
his attacker.

*A ghostly security gate comes down, trapping the blurry
figure inside the gallery.*

FACHE
No. He locked his attacker *out.*

*The blurry attacker disappears and reappears on the
other side of the security gate, now trapped outside.*

FACHE
Unfortunately he could not lock out
his bullets as well.

*The blurry figure now aims at ghostly Sauniere and fires.
Sauniere stumbles backwards, hit in the stomach.*

FACHE
Gunshot residue on the bars.

*As the ghostly attacker flees straight through our two men,
Langdon follows Fache through vanishing bars into . . .*

A, LANGDON'S P.O.V. - A GHOSTLY SAUNIERE RUNS
OUT OF HIS OFFICE.

D, THE SECURITY GATE FALLS IN FRONT OF LANGDON
AND FACHE, TRAPPING THE BLURRY GHOST.   TRACK
LANGDON"
"HE ACTIVATED THE SECURITY GATE TO TRAP
HIS ATTACKER ? "

B, CAMERA DOLLIES BACK AND PANS TO FOLLOW
SAUNIERE PAST LANGDON, LANGDON WATCHES
HIM GO BY, A BLURRY GHOST FOLLOWS.   DOLLY
AND
PAN

"NO. HE LOCKED HIS ATTACKER OUT" IN
THE HALLWAY."
THE BLURRY GHOST DISAPPEARS AND REAPPEARS ON
THEIR SIDE OF THE GATE.

C, CAMERA CONTINUES TO PAN WITH
SAUNIERE AND THEN TRACKS TO
FOLLOW ALL FOUR TO THE GRAND
GALLERY.   PAN
AND
TRACK

FACHE "
"UNFORTUNATELY, HE COULD NOT LOCK OUT
HIS BULLETS AS WELL."   43

INT. LOUVRE GRANDE GALERIE – CONTINUOUS
Langdon can now see the body on the floor. Naked and
spread-eagle, holding a black pen. Around the corpse,
wide circles of blood, and on his stomach a red and drip-
ping pentagram.

LANGDON

Dear God.

FACHE

No, Mr. Langdon. I would say quite the
opposite, wouldn't you?

EXT. G4 – NIGHT
The sleek jet skims over moonlit clouds.

INT. G4 – NIGHT
A MAN sits staring out at the full moon. See his face
reflected in the Plexiglas, nose once broken, hard eyes.

VOICE (over)

Your Eminence . . .

He turns across the table to face a fresh, sharp-eyed
CLERIC. The older man smiles. This is BISHOP
ARINGAROSA.

A STEWARDESS with a cross hanging low around her
neck serves tea. Monitors scroll CNN headlines, CNBC
financial news.

Storyboards by Robert Ballantyne.

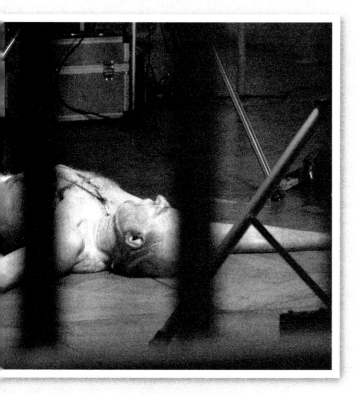

ARINGAROSA
We are a simple Catholic church.

CLERIC
Simple? With a brand new $47 million residence in Manhattan?

ARINGAROSA
Our followers are supportive. Should we apologize for that?

CLERIC
Perhaps a less defensive tack, Your Eminence? The press conference will be widely attended.

Aringarosa nods, tries a softer TONE.

ARINGAROSA
We are not cafeteria Catholics, picking and choosing which rules we follow. We follow doctrine rigorously.

The cleric nods.

ARINGAROSA
You may proceed, son.

CLERIC
Many call Opus Dei a brainwashing cult. Others, an ultra-conservative Christian secret society.

CLERIC
Does doctrine necessarily include vows of chastity, tithing, and atonement for sins through self-flagellation and the cilice?

ARINGAROSA
Thousands of our members are married, have families. Only a small portion choose lives of asceticism in our cloistered residence halls. All strive to better the world by doing God's work. Surely this is an admirable way to lead one's life.

QUICK MATCH DISSOLVE

A, QUICK DISSOLVE TO INT. JET - MOON IN SAME POSITION,
VOICE COVER):
"YOUR EMINENCE..."

B, CAMERA PULLS BACK AND ADJUSTS AS
BISHOP ARINGAROSA TURNS INTO C.U.
ARINGAROSA:
"YOU MAY PROCEED."

PULL BACK

45

CLERIC
Some media are referring to Opus Dei as God's Mafia. Why is that?

ARINGAROSA
I suppose people fear what they do not understand.

Something changes in the Bishop's eyes.

ARINGAROSA
Or perhaps this war finally draws to a close.

The young man is startled.

CLERIC
Bishop?

That is when Aringarosa's seat phone RINGS.

ARINGAROSA
That will do for today, Carlos.

The cleric nods, gone to the back of the plane like a shadow.

ARINGAROSA
(into the phone)
Yes?

TEACHER (over)
Silas has succeeded. The legend is true.
It hides beneath the rose.

The familiar WHISPER, again in Latin.

TEACHER (over)
Now, Bishop, I need you to make a
phone call for me.

Aringarosa closes his eyes with sublime relief.

INT. LOUVRE GRANDE GALERIE – NIGHT
Langdon stands over the dead man, taking in the tableau.

LANGDON
Jesus, this is the Vitruvian Man.

Fache is watching Langdon closely.

LANGDON
He's positioned his body to duplicate
one of Leonardo Da Vinci's most famous
sketches. It's on a one-euro coin.

FACHE
And why would he do that?

Langdon fingers a coin. Kneels, looking at the corpse's
fingertip, which is red and dark.

LANGDON
Wait. He drew this with his own blood?

FACHE
From the bullet hole.

Fache's expression is grim.

FACHE
Stomach wounds leave one ample time to die.

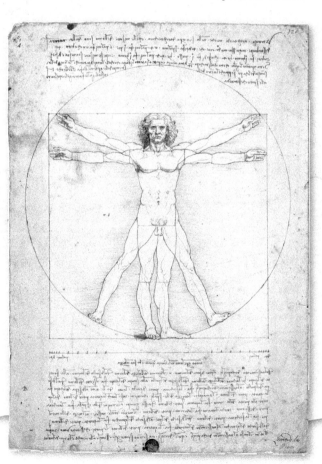

The Vitruvian Man

This image, central to both Da Vinci's work and
Dan Brown's novel, offers the first major clue
in *The Da Vinci Code*. For the film, a life-cast
of actor Jean-Pierre Marielle (in the role of Sauniere,
left-hand page) was rendered in rubber
and substituted for the actor during
much of the lengthy filming process.

47

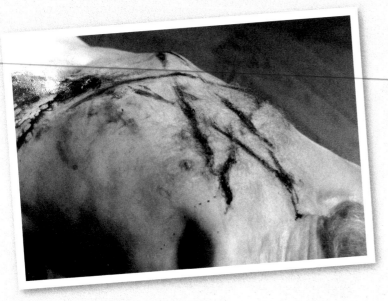

FACHE
Yes. Devil worship.

LANGDON
No, no. The pentacle before that. It's the symbol for Venus. It represents the female half of things — the concept called "the divine goddess" by religious historians.

FACHE
You are telling me Sauniere's last act on earth was to draw a goddess symbol on his stomach? Why?

Something too interrogative about the way he says it.

LANGDON
Captain Fache. Obviously I can't tell you why Mr. Sauniere drew that symbol or placed his body this way or is clutching that marking pen in his hand . . .

Fache glances at the stylus, a detail he had yet to mention.

LANGDON
Poor old man.

FACHE
Quite so. And the star on his skin?

LANGDON
The pentacle.

There is something suddenly dogged in the Frenchman's tone.

FACHE
And its meaning?

LANGDON
The pentacle's ancient. Symbols carry different meanings in different settings. Just tonight I was giving a lecture —

FACHE
This symbol, Professor.

LANGDON
Okay. The pentacle is a pagan religious icon.

LANGDON

But he, as well as anyone, would know this symbol's meaning. And it has nothing to do with worshiping the devil.

FACHE

Is that so?

LANGDON

Yes.

Fache is walking around the body. He lifts a penlight off the desk, turns it on, tip spilling a glowing, purple beam.

FACHE

Then what do you make of this?

Fache shines the light on the floor, revealing purple letters appearing in the directed ultraviolet glow.

13 – 3 – 2 – 21 – 1 – 1 – 8 – 5
O, Draconian devil!
Oh, lame saint!

Langdon goes down on his haunches, inspects the stylus.

LANGDON

Ultraviolet ink. Used for tagging paintings for restoration.

FACHE

What would *you* do if you had such limited time to send a message?

LANGDON

. . . I suppose I'd try to identify my killer.

FACHE

Précisément.

Fache smiles at Langdon. Think shark and its kill.

FACHE

Précisément. So, Professor —

WOMAN'S VOICE (over)

Excusez-moi, Commissaire.

A young WOMAN is approaching down the long hall with a police escort. She has a case folder in her hand.

SOPHIE

Please pardon the interruption but —

FACHE

C'est pas le moment —

SOPHIE

I received the crime scene jpegs at headquarters. I've deciphered the code. It is a Fibonacci sequence.

FACHE
La suite de Fibonacci?

SOPHIE
Oui. **The numbers are only out of order.**

Langdon's eyes narrow; how the hell did he miss that?

LANGDON
Ow. It is the Fibonacci sequence. From
the top of the order, too.

Sophie hands Fache a sheet of paper from the case file.

SOPHIE
Commissaire, I will explain. *But I just
have a message for . . .*
(*turning to Langdon*)
Professor Langdon, right?
(*to Fache*)
I get the impression it's urgent.
(*to Langdon*)
I am Sophie Neveu, DCPJ Cryptology.
Your embassy called Division.

She hands Langdon a scrap of paper.

SOPHIE
I'm sorry, monsieur. They said it was a
matter of life and death.

Her gaze, so intense, almost vibrating.

SOPHIE
This is the number of your embassy's
messaging service.

LANGDON
I don't have a cell phone.

Fache hands over his mobile phone.

FACHE
Use mine.

Langdon steps away and dials the phone as the two
police TALK excitedly in FRENCH in the background.

PHONE (*Sophie's voice*)
Vous êtes bien chez Sophie Neveu —

Langdon looks up at Sophie, who is rearranging the
numbers for Fache on a piece of paper.

LANGDON
Ms. Neveu. You gave me —

Sophie's response is too fast, as if anticipating him.

SOPHIE
No. That's the right number. The
embassy has an automated message
system. You have to dial an access
code to pick up your messages.

LANGDON
Look, I'm getting your —

SOPHIE
It's the three-digit code. It's on the paper I gave you.

Before she looks back at Fache, the message she sends Langdon with her eyes is clear. Do what I say. Langdon frowns, tapping in the numbers.

PHONE (*Sophie's voice*)
Mr. Langdon. Do not react to this message. Just listen calmly. You must follow my directions very closely. You are in great danger.

EXT. CHURCH OF SAINT-SULPICE – NIGHT
A mighty Gothic structure. WIND blows. (OVER) A PHONE.

INT. CHURCH OF SAINT-SULPICE – PARIS – NIGHT
A small room. Stone floors. Bed, Bible, hot plate. Single window open to the autumn air. (OVER) The phone RINGS on.

An elderly WOMAN'S hand reaches out from bed to answer. She sits up groggily. SISTER SANDRINE BIEIL.

SANDRINE
Eglise Saint-Sulpice.

Sandrine listens a beat, her expression darkening.

SANDRINE
Of course, Father. But so late?
Wouldn't tomorrow . . . ?

Sandrine listens some more.

SANDRINE
It would be my pleasure.

Sandrine stands, pulling her robe around sixty-year-old bones, meager comfort against the cool night air.

BANG! The window SLAMS shut.

Sandrine spins, crossing herself. She stands there, still, trying to shake off a sudden, surprising fear.

INT. LOUVRE GRANDE GALERIE – NIGHT
Langdon hands Fache back his cell phone. Fache is staring after Sophie as she departs down the hall.

FACHE
(off his head)
Too much up here.

LANGDON
There's been an accident. A friend. I need to fly home in the morning.

FACHE
I see.

LANGDON
Is there a bathroom I can use? I just need to splash my face.

FACHE
Of course. They are back the way we came.

LANGDON
Aren't there closer ones up ahead?

Fache's eyes narrow. Langdon is right.

FACHE
Yes.

Fache holds up the paper on which Sophie has rearranged the numbers to form the Fibonacci sequence.

FACHE
She said it's meaningless. A mathematical joke.

Fache isn't moving. He holds Langdon's eyes.

FACHE
Is it meaningless?

Langdon steps around him.

LANGDON
I'll have another look when I get back.

FACHE
I am sorry, of course.

But there is little sorrow in Fache's eyes as he watches Langdon go. He balls up the paper, tosses it on the floor.

INT./EXT. BLACK AUDI – PARIS – NIGHT
Silas pulls in front of floodlit Saint-Sulpice. He closes his eyes to pray.

SILAS
(in Spanish)
Christ, give me strength.

On the windscreen, the past takes form. A man beats a woman viciously, the two SHOUTING at each other in Spanish. Young Silas grabs a knife, plunges it into his father's back. The man is still trying to free the blade as he dies.

SILAS
(in Spanish)
Christ, give me strength.

Young Silas sits in a prison cell beside stacks of books as the years pass, Silas aging into an adult before our eyes, becoming as transparent as a ghost.

SILAS
(in Spanish)
Christ, give me strength.

The nighttime world of his cell is turned upside down, walls crumbling as he is thrown out of bed; scrambling out of the broken prison, past bodies; stumbling on the road until he falls, looks up to realize he has collapsed on the steps of a church, world going black in the burning sun.

SILAS
(in Spanish)
Christ, give me strength.

Jesus stares kindly down on him; light, dark, light again; male hands bear soup, bread. Finally, beneath the crucifix over his bed, the face of Silas's human savior. Aringarosa.

SILAS
(in Spanish)
Christ, give me strength.

Silas in his small room. (OVER) SHOUTS, STRUGGLE. He emerges to see Aringarosa being beaten by a thief caught in the act. A stomp to Aringarosa's face snaps his nose. The thief arches backwards, eyes rolling as blood spills from his throat. Silas stands behind him, knife in hand. Silas cradles the fallen priest.

SILAS
(in Spanish)
Christ, give me strength.

Silas opens his eyes. He climbs out, going to the church. As he crosses the street, LINGER on a circular brass marker set in the pavement.

INT. LOUVRE – BATHROOM – NIGHT
CLOSE on a BAR OF SOAP. Langdon ENTERS in the mirror above. Sophie Neveu is waiting. The two stare at each other.

SOPHIE
So what happened?

LANGDON
What's going on?

SOPHIE
Do you have a message from Sauniere?

LANGDON
What are you talking about?

The two stare at each other a beat. Sophie shakes her head.

SOPHIE
Crazy old man.

LANGDON
Look, you've got me confused with someone else. I was asked to come here to consult —

That very French EXHALE, half laugh, half exasperation.

SOPHIE
No. You are *sous surveillance cachée.*

LANGDON
Yes. Of course — I'm what?

She is frustrated, wants to get answers not give them.

SOPHIE
Bring the suspect to the crime scene, and hope he incriminates himself.

LANGDON
Suspect? How could I be a suspect?

She taps her hip pockets.

SOPHIE
Check your jacket pocket.

Langdon simply stares at her like she's a lunatic.

SOPHIE
So? Just look.

Langdon obliges. Fingers brush something unexpected. From his pocket he removes a metallic, button-sized disk.

SOPHIE

GPS tracking dot. Accurate within two feet anywhere on the globe. The agent who picked you up slipped it into your jacket. In case you tried to run. We have you on a little leash, Professor.

INT. CURATOR'S OFFICE – FLASH CUT

ON a laptop SCREEN a floor plan schematic, a red dot blinking over the text: TOILETTES PUBLIQUES.

INT. LOUVRE – BATHROOM – NIGHT

Langdon is ogling the small transceiver.

LANGDON

Why would I run? I didn't do anything.

SOPHIE

Fache isn't even looking for other suspects, okay? He is sure you are guilty.

LANGDON

Think clearly here. There's no logical basis for that.

SOPHIE

So, what do you think about the fourth line of text Fache wiped clean before you arrived?

De: COLLET@dcpj.fr
Objet: **FW: Scène du crime - message à déchiffrer**
Date: Aujourd'hui 20:30
A: NEVEU@crypt.fr, NICOLAS@crypt.fr, VERGES@crypt.fr, PERRINE@crypt.fr,
FERREIRA@crypt.fr, FREZET@crypt.fr, HUNAULT@crypt.fr
Pièces jointes: jpg. 200KB.

La note: Nous avons besoin de déchiffrer de façon urgente le message dans les pièces jointes. Ce
message a été trouvé sur la scène du crime, à côté de Jacques Saunière.
De: COLLET@dcpj.fr
Date: Aujourd'hui 20:30
A: ANSELME@crypt.fr
Objet: **Scène du crime - message à déchiffrer**

She is already taking a small glossy from her sweater.

> *13 – 3 – 2 – 21 – 1 – 1 – 8 – 5*
> *O, Draconian devil!*
> *Oh, lame saint!*
> *P.S. Find Robert Langdon.*

HOLD on Langdon. Stunned.

INT. CHURCH OF SAINT-SULPICE – NIGHT – WALKING
Cavernous. Silas follows SISTER SANDRINE BIEIL
into the immense, empty sanctuary. The nun hugs her
habit close.

> SANDRINE
> You have powerful friends. The bishop
> of Opus Dei himself called our Father
> to request this tour.

> SILAS
> Bishop Aringarosa has been . . . kind to me.

Something she doesn't like here. Maybe just being awo-
ken so late into the night. Maybe something more.

> SILAS
> I could not miss this chance to pray
> inside the Saint-Sulpice.

> SANDRINE
> *(off the oculus)*
> A pity you could not wait for morning.
> The light is not ideal —

> SILAS
> My plane leaves early. Tell me of the
> rose line, please?

Sandrine has repeated these words again and again.

> SANDRINE
> A rose line, also called a meridian or
> longitude, is any line from the North to
> South poles.

Embedded in the floor, a thin polished strip of brass
glistens. The line bears graduated markings, like
a ruler.

> SANDRINE
> Early navigators had to choose which
> of these lines would be *the* rose line,
> the zero longitude.

Silas follows the brass strip with his eyes as it crosses the
floor, slices the main altar, cleaves the communion rail,
and arrives at the base of an odd Egyptian obelisk.

> SANDRINE
> Today that line is in Greenwich,
> England. But 135 brass markers set
> into the streets of Paris mark the

ABOVE: The Saint-Sulpice set, before and after digital enhancement.
BELOW: The actual Saint-Sulpice altar in Paris.

Re-creating Saint-Sulpice

The scenes set in Saint-Sulpice were among the most complicated re-creations in the film. All exteriors were shot at night, on location outside the historic church in Paris. All interiors were generated from a partial set built in Shepperton Studios. A section of the church containing the gnomon, altar, and pews was built and surrounded by walls of green screens. Later, overseen by VFX (visual effects) supervisor Angus Bickerton, a fully digital environment was built within a computer, rendered, and used to replace the green screens in post-production.

world's first prime meridian, which
passed through this very church.

On the ancient floor, another of those brass markers.

SILAS

It hides beneath the rose.

SANDRINE

I'm sorry?

They have reached the front pew. Silas turns to
face her.

SILAS

Sister. I kept you long enough. I can
show myself out.

SANDRINE

Oh, I hardly sleep these days —

Silas lays his hand on her shoulder, his flesh like ice.

SILAS

I insist. May the peace of the Lord be
with you.

Those eyes. It takes her a moment to answer.

SANDRINE

And with you.

HOLD on Silas as he watches her go.

SOPHIE (over)

Fache will be in here soon. You can't
think of any message he left for me?

INT. LOUVRE – BATHROOM – NIGHT
Langdon stares at the photo in his hand.

LANGDON

Fache?

SOPHIE

Sauniere.

Sophie takes back the photo.

LANGDON

Only that we meet.

SOPHIE

That you meet *me*?

LANGDON

No, *him*. Sauniere.

Langdon clocks the flicker of emotion in her eyes.

LANGDON

You knew him.

SOPHIE

When did he contact you? Today?

LANGDON
Yes.

SOPHIE
What time? *What time?*

LANGDON
Around three, I think.

Sophie nods, eyes closing, something confirmed here.

SOPHIE
The gallery alarm was triggered at
eight. You were . . . ?

LANGDON
I was giving a lecture.

SOPHIE
At *nine*. You had the privacy light on
in your hotel until eight-thirty, right?

LANGDON
Huh.

SOPHIE
We call Fache the Bull. Once he starts, he
doesn't stop. He can arrest you and detain
you for months while he builds a case —

LANGDON
Ms. Neveu —

SOPHIE
— By then whatever Sauniere wanted
you to tell me will be useless.

LANGDON
Lady, stop. Just stop!

Strength in his VOICE gets through.

LANGDON
Who are you? What are you talking
about? Tell you what?

SOPHIE
Maybe who really killed him.

What he sees in her face is unexpected. A terrible sadness.

SOPHIE
The Fibonacci sequence, I believe
Sauniere wrote it so this investigation
would include cryptographers. That
way I would learn quickly of his death.

LANGDON
That's quite a leap.

SOPHIE
Not so. And the letters, P.S. . . .

LANGDON

Post Script.

SOPHIE

Princesse Sophie. Princess Sophie.

Sad smile at the past.

SOPHIE

Oh, silly, I know. But I was only a girl
when I lived with him.

He looks up. A slight smile at his misunderstanding.

SOPHIE

Jacques Sauniere was my grandfather.
Apparently it was his dying wish that
we meet. If you help me understand

why, I will get you to your embassy
where we cannot arrest you.

She holds his eyes.

SOPHIE

Or else explain to Fache why your
name is on the floor. And your alibi at
the time of the murder.

LANGDON

Fache isn't going to just let me stroll
out the front door, is he?

SOPHIE

No. If we are to get away from here,
we must find another way.

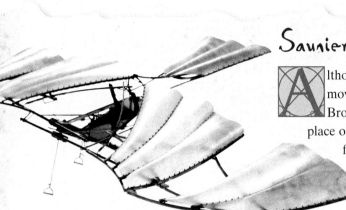

Sauniere's Desk

Although never mentioned in the movie, the model knight from Dan Brown's novel appears in its proper place on Sauniere's desk. Da Vinci's flying machine hangs from the office ceiling.

Langdon splashes his face in the sink, resting the GPS dot near the bar of soap.

> **LANGDON**
> All right, your highness. What exactly do you propose?

Sophie climbs a low heater, Paris twinkling out the window. He looks up at her.

> **SOPHIE**
> No. We'll break our necks.

INT. LOUVRE – CURATOR'S OFFICE
TILT DOWN past a hanging Da Vinci flying machine into this small room overflowing with books. Fache and his men gather around a laptop. ON THE LAPTOP SCREEN: that same blinking red dot.

> **FACHE**
> He's still in there?

Collet is on the phone.

> **FACHE**
> Collet? What's he doing in there?

Collet gestures to the phone. Fache just shakes his head, looks down at an open book by the base of a robotic knight.

BOOK–CLOSE. That text of Langdon's, open to a lattice-like diagram over which Sauniere has written simple words.

> **FACHE**
> Blood trail.
> *(turning)*
> Collet. Get off the phone.

Collet hangs up, his expression darkening.

> **COLLET**
> Crypto. They called to say they identified the code.

> **FACHE**
> Neveu told us already. I should have fired her on the spot, barging in like that —

Collet shakes his head.

61

COLLET
Yes. Except, they didn't send Neveu.

FACHE
What?

COP
(urgent)
Commissaire!

ON THE LAPTOP SCREEN: the red blinking dot is moving.

COLLET
He's going for the window ledge.

FACHE
Absurd. It's too high —

The dot is suddenly outside the building's perimeter.

FACHE
What's going on? Is he still — ? Shit.

A cop fumbles with the controls and the screen shifts, now showing a Paris street map. The dot is no longer moving.

COLLET
He jumped.

INT. LOUVRE – GRANDE GALERIE – RUNNING
Fache is sprinting down the Grande Galerie. The radio on his belt growls with STATIC, begins spitting WORDS.

RADIO (Collet's voice)
He's moving again. Too fast. He must be in a car.

Fache BANGS into . . .

INT. LOUVRE BATHROOM – CONTINUOUS
Fache flies across the empty room to the open window.

RADIO (Collet's voice)
He's going south. Crossing the Seine on Pont du Carrousel.

Fache pushes himself up, body going halfway out the window as he peers into the night.

FACHE-POV. The only vehicle on Pont du Carrousel is an enormous twin-bed Trailor delivery truck.

RADIO (Collet's voice)
Turning. Right on Quai Voltaire!

FACHE-POV. Sure enough, the truck is slowing down and making a wide right onto Quai Voltaire.

FACHE
Fumier.

Behind the Cameras

Ron Howard scouting shots with Sal Totino (*above and right*); reviewing a special effect with Angus Bickerton and Tom Hanks (*right*). Brian Grazer, Sony chairman and CEO Michael Lynton, and Candide Franklyn (*lower right*); Todd Hallowell, Tom Hanks, and Sony Pictures chairman, Amy Pascal (*bottom right*). Ron Howard working a scene with Annie Penn, Tom Hanks, Audrey Tautou, Akiva Goldsman, Bill Connor, and Candide Franklyn (*below*).

EXT. LOUVRE – NIGHT – MINUTES LATER
Cop cars are pulling away from the building, bubble
lights flashing. PULL BACK TO REVEAL . . .

INT. LOUVRE MAIN GALLERY – NIGHT
Sophie and Langdon stand in shadows peering out a
window. A lone remaining COP walks away, heading
down the stairs.

> **SOPHIE**
> You have quite a good throwing arm
> for a professor, Professor.

They are heading down the corridor towards a lighted
exit sign. Something has caught Sophie's eye. She slows.

> **SOPHIE**
> It will take Fache a few minutes to
> realize you are not on that truck.

There, in the archway, Sauniere's body.

> **SOPHIE**
> That cop will check the whole lower
> floor. I would only take a moment.

Langdon understands her in an instant.

> **LANGDON**
> Of course.

INT. LOUVRE GRANDE GALERIE – SECONDS LATER
Sophie is kneeling by the old man, his face so still.

> **SOPHIE**
> He is much older than I remember.

Langdon stands a few feet off, watching her.

> **SOPHIE**
> I hadn't seen or spoken to him in a
> very long time.

*Sophie looks up. In the corner, her grandfather towers over
her younger self, his hand raised, as if about to strike.*

> **SOPHIE**
> Still, he tried to call me each year. On
> my birthday.

She touches soft, still flesh.

SOPHIE
Such productions when I was a girl, my birthdays. Puzzles. Codes. Always a treasure hunt just to find my gift at the end.

In her mix of emotions, a tenderness here that surprises her.

SOPHIE
He phoned my office today. Several times. He said it was a matter of life and death. I thought it was another trick to get back in touch.

More than sadness, now. Guilt.

SOPHIE
When I wouldn't take his calls, he even came to the station. I wasn't there at the time. Around two PM.

She glances up at him.

LANGDON
An hour before he e-mailed me.

SOPHIE
Yes. It seems, when he couldn't speak to me, he reached out to you, instead.

The heaviness she feels is unexpected.

SOPHIE
Whatever he needed so badly to say, he found neither of us in time.

A last touch. As Sophie rises, Langdon notices something on the floor. A familiar ball of paper. Langdon stops cold.

SOPHIE
Professor?

LANGDON
Come on. It can't be that easy.

Langdon has lifted the paper, shaking his head, already moving back towards the body.

LANGDON
Fibonacci numbers only have meaning in their correct order.

Langdon lifts the UV penlight left on the floor, illuminates and kneels over the message.

LANGDON
These were scrambled.

The numbers move, sliding upward on the floor and finding a different order to become the famous Fibonacci sequence.

LANGDON

You said Sauniere liked codes. What if the scrambled numbers are a clue? A cipher to decode the rest of the message.

Langdon pulls a leather pad and pen from his jacket, stares at the text on the floor.

LANGDON
(to himself)
O, Draconian devil. Oh, lame saint. Meaningless . . .

Now the letters start to move, shifting in sequence, finding and fixing some words, violently rejecting others.

LANGDON

Unless you assume these letters are out of order too.

SOPHIE

An anagram.

The words are coming and going faster and faster. Sophie's eyes narrow as she registers his impossible focus.

SOPHIE

You have eidetic memory?

LANGDON

Not quite. But I pretty much remember what I see —
(beat)
Whoa. Anagram is right.

Langdon scribbles on his pad, hands it to Sophie.

Leonardo Da Vinci
The Mona Lisa

SOPHIE

Professor. The Mona Lisa is right over here.

INT. CHURCH OF SAINT-SULPICE – BALCONY

Hiding in the balcony shadows, Sandrine watches Silas carry a heavy iron candle-holder from the altar, following the rose line to the giant obelisk at its terminus.

Silas looks up towards the residential quarters. Sandrine leans back, willing herself invisible.

Silas slips off his cowl. He wraps the cloth over the rod.

Sandrine watches Silas drive the silenced lance again and again until tiles below him SHATTER.

INT. CHURCH OF SAINT-SULPICE – SANCTUARY – CONTINUOUS

Silas is on his knees, hungrily tearing away jagged pieces of stone from the opening, revealing the hidden compartment below. He reaches in with a pale arm. First nothing. Then . . .

From within, Silas pulls an old stone tablet, rough-hewn and engraved with the simplest of inscriptions.

Job 38:11.

INT. LOUVRE – SALLE DES ETATS
Langdon walks fast, Sophie trailing at a clip.

> **LANGDON**
> Okay. Sfumato shading. Smile in low spatial frequencies. Horizon line on the left significantly lower than on the right.

They have reached a glass case in the center of the room.

> **SOPHIE**
> Why?

> **LANGDON**
> See. It makes her appear larger from the left than the right. Historically, the left is female and right is male.

> **SOPHIE**
> The sacred feminine?

Sophie is already examining the painting's case. Doesn't see Langdon's puzzled reaction.

> **LANGDON**
> Why do you say that?

> **SOPHIE**
> Something my grandfather said the first time we came here.

Langdon seems about to speak. But Sophie has found something.

> **SOPHIE**
> There.

On the floor, a cluster of several tiny red drops.

> **SOPHIE**
> Blood.

Sophie finds her own UV penlight, shines the beam on the glass, letters appearing in a single, scrawled sentence.

SOPHIE
(reading)
So Dark The Con Of Man.

LANGDON
. . . No. It doesn't say that.

Langdon has pushed closer, now stares at the glowing text. These words mean something to him.

SOPHIE
Is it another anagram? Can you break it?

(OVER) Somewhere downstairs a door SLAMS.

SOPHIE
Professor, hurry —

He locks on the text. His words come incredibly fast.

LANGDON
Man-mad-mark-corks-rocks —

Sophie spins, fixing on a painting on the opposite wall.

SOPHIE
Madonna of the Rocks.

She crosses. The painting is askew. Sophie grabs the frame.

LANGDON
Don't —

She jerks the painting half from the wall. Something drops to the floor in the dim light. A hanging, silver cruciform.

LANGDON
This can't be this.

(OVER) FOOTSTEPS. Sophie and Langdon lock eyes.

EXT. PARIS – BANK OF THE SEINE – NIGHT
A DRIVER PROTESTS as a familiar truck is searched by a swarm of DCPJ officers, all finding no joy. PULL BACK . . .

Fache stands staring at his cell phone, scrolling through dialed numbers. He presses the most recent.

> PHONE
> *Vous êtes bien chez Sophie Neveu —*

> FACHE
> *(hanging up)*
> *Merde.*

Collet has crossed the moonlit street, hands something to Fache. A bar of soap, shiny transponder dug inside.

> COLLET
> **He must have thrown it from the window. Smart to hit the truck.**

Fache hangs up, his expression dark as night.

> FACHE
> **What, you admire him now?**

Collet raises an eyebrow. Fache is driven, even for Fache.

> FACHE
> **We are idiots. Who did we leave at the museum? Ledoux? Get him on the radio.**

INT. LOUVRE – SALLE DES ETATS – NIGHT
A cop enters to find Langdon and Sophie, the painting on the floor between them.

> COP
> *Arretez.* **You are under arrest. Step away. Put the painting down.**

She's got the five-foot-tall *Madonna on the Rocks*, held out in front of her.

> SOPHIE
> **No! Put down your gun. Right now.**

The cop has his gun trained on her. Sophie begins pushing her knee into the back of the canvas. The cop hesitates.

> SOPHIE
> **Slide the gun and radio to me. Move quickly. I never liked this painting much. Do it!**

A long beat. The guard obliges. Sophie grabs the pistol.

> FACHE *(over)*
> **Two suspects. Maybe still in the museum.**

Sophie kicks the radio to Langdon. (OVER) Fache's VOICE CRACKLES.

> FACHE *(over)*
> **They should be considered armed and dangerous.**

Sophie lets the painting fall, the cop rushing to grab it.

SOPHIE

Run!

They race, fast, to the door.

SOPHIE
(off the gun)
Don't follow us.

They run out the door.

Parlez-vous Français?

ot only does *The Da Vinci Code* boast an international cast of actors; lines in the movie are spoken in four different languages. As such, English dialogue appeared on script pages, and other language translations appeared on vellum pages overlaying the original dialogue.

Song Sung Blue Revisions 20/09/05 35.

40   INT. LOUVRE — SALLE DES ETATS — NIGHT   40

A cop enters to find Langdon and Sophie, the painting on the floor between them.

COP
Police! Restez où vous êtes. Posez-
le tableau. Et écartez-vous. down.

She's got the five foot tall Madonna on the Rocks, held out in front of her.

SOPHIE
Non. Vous, vous posez votre arme. Sinon je l'éclate
votre tableau. Allez, depechez-vous.

The Cop has his gun trained on her. Sophie begins pushing her knee into the back of the canvas. The Cop hesitates.

SOPHIE
Faites glisser votre arme et le talkie
aussi very moi. J'ai jamais trop aime
cette peinture moi. Allez.

A long beat. The Guard obliges. Sophie grabs the pistol.

FACHE (OVER)
Deux suspects, ils sont sans the

38   CONTINUED: (2)   34.

LANGDON
Man-mad mark-corks-rocks.

Sophie spins, fixing on a painting on the opposite wall.

SOPHIE
Madonna of the Rocks.

She crosses. The painting is askew. Sophie grabs the frame.

LANGDON
Don't-

She jerks the painting half from the wall. Something drops to the floor in the dim light. A hanging, silver crucifix.

LANGDON
This can't be this.

(OVER) FOOTSTEPS. Sophie and Langdon lock eyes.

EXT. PARIS — BANKS OF THE SEINE — NIGHT

A DRIVER PROTESTS as a familiar truck is searched by a swarm of DCPJ officers, all finding no joy. PULL BACK...

Fache stands staring at his cell phone, scrolling through dialed numbers. He presses the most recent.

PHONE
Vous êtes bien chez Sophie Neveu-

FACHE
(hanging up)
Merde.

Collet has crossed the moonlit street, hands something to Fache. A bar of soap, shiny transponder dug inside.

COLLET
Il a dû le jeter par la fenêtre. Pile
dans le camion. Pas maladroit ce mec.

Fache hangs up, his expression dark as night.

FACHE
Quoi, vous l'admirez maintenant ?

Collet raises an eyebrow. Fache is driven, even for Fache.

FACHE
On est des imbéciles. On a laissé
qui au musée ? Ledoux ? Appelez-
le radio.

INT. LOUVRE MUSEUM – NIGHT – HIGH ANGLE
Sophie and Langdon flee past statuary down steep stairs
as they toss gun and radio away into the shadows.

INT. CHURCH OF SAINT-SULPICE – RESIDENCE – NIGHT
Sister Sandrine sits on her bed, phone to her ear, an aged
envelope torn hastily open on the bedspread beside her.

On the small phone table lies an equally yellowed piece
of paper, a fleur-de-lis as its only moniker.

Three out of four Paris phone numbers on the paper have
been shakily crossed out. Sandrine's face is deadly pale.

> **PHONE** (*over*)
> **This is Jacques Sauniere. Please leave
> a message after the tone.**

> **SANDRINE**
> **Please, monsieur. Please pick up. I
> have called the list. I fear the others
> are dead. The lie has been told. The
> floor panel has been broken. Please,
> sir. You must answer if you are there.**

> **SILAS** (*over*)
> Job 38:11. Do you know it, Sister?

Sandrine stands up in fear to face Silas in the doorway.
He still holds the stone tablet. She puts down the phone.

> **SANDRINE**
> Job 38:11: *Hitherto shalt thou come, but
> no further.*

> **SILAS**
> But no further. Do you mock me?
> Where is the keystone?

> **SANDRINE**
> I don't know.

He stares at her. Knows her words are true.

> **SILAS**
> You are a sister of the Church and yet
> you serve *them*?

> **SANDRINE**
> Jesus had but one true message.

> **SILAS**
> Yes.

Silas swings fast, SNAPPING her neck with the old stone.
Even before she hits the bed, her eyes are wide and staring.

> **SILAS**
> (*kneeling, in Latin*)
> Come, you Saints of God; hasten,
> Angels of the Lord . . .

EXT. CASTLE GANDOLFO – ITALY – NIGHT
A Fiat pulls up before an immense Gothic castle, two huge
metal telescope-domes built into the ancient stone roof.

SILAS *(over)*
(in Latin)
To receive her soul and bring her to
the sight of the Almighty . . .

**INT. CASTLE GANDOLFO – BIBLIOTECA
ASTRONOMICA – NIGHT**
A vast square room of dark wood bookcases from floor to
ceiling, all covered in books. Over twenty-five thousand.

VOICE *(over)*
Welcome, Bishop.

Aringarosa ENTERS to face a MAN at a long boardroom
table, a crystal decanter breathing red before him.

ARINGAROSA
Most Reverent Prefect.

The PREFECT rises, a man of impossible girth.

PREFECT
It's been too long, Manuel. I saw your
press conference. Very . . . priestly.

ARINGAROSA
Vultures. But you need a good cover to fly to
Italy these days. So how are things in Rome?

PREFECT
We serve at His pleasure.

Aringarosa's smile does not belie the contempt in his eyes.

ARINGAROSA
Today is today. But there are many tomorrows.

Something old about these words. The Prefect rises,
gestures to the decanter.

PREFECT
Vatican cellars. 1976.

ARINGAROSA
A year of independence. How fitting.

PREFECT
I thought you'd like it. I'll fetch the others.

EXT. LOUVRE MUSEUM – NIGHT
(OVER) SIRENS. Squad cars descend on the museum,
bubble lights flashing, spilling cops. PULL BACK . . .

INT. SMART CAR – PARIS STREET – DRIVING – NIGHT
Sophie drives, nervous, the police assault on the museum
diminishing in the mirror.

SOPHIE
It was his.

She lifts the cross, dangling from the chain in her hand.

SOPHIE
I remember finding it once when I was a girl.
He promised he'd give it to me one day.

Something dark in her eyes.

SOPHIE
He was one for promises, my grandfather.

Langdon glances at the engraved flower on the cross.

LANGDON
Have you ever heard those words before, Sophie? *So dark the con of man?*

SOPHIE
No. Have you?

LANGDON
When you were a child . . . Were you ever aware of any gatherings? Anything ritualistic in nature? Strange meetings or ceremonies? Any gatherings he might have wanted kept secret? Did he ever talk about something called the Priory of Sion?

SOPHIE
The what? Why are you asking these things?

Langdon takes a breath before answering.

LANGDON
The Priory of Sion is a myth. One of the oldest and most secret societies, with leaders like Sir Isaac Newton, and Leonardo himself. Guardians of one of history's greatest secrets, a secret they supposedly refer to as "the dark con of man."

SOPHIE
What secret?

Langdon shakes his head.

LANGDON
It's a myth. The Priory is history's version of Santa Claus. Santa has his house at the North Pole, his reindeer and his flying sleigh. The Priory has their oath, their chalice, their crest of fleur-de-lis — which they share, by the way, with the New Orleans Saints and Kappa-Kappa-Gamma.

SOPHIE
This flower is a fleur-de-lis.

LANGDON
Yes. That's supposedly the seal of their secret brotherhood.

Ext. Paris – Car – Moving

Action sequences in the screenplay will often be described concisely, and then expand once stunt and special effects departments begin to apply their craft. In *The Da Vinci Code*, a dozen-line car chase generated over one hundred storyboards and many days of filming.

SOPHIE

What is this secret they were supposed
to be guarding?

LANGDON

Well, how does one say this, the Priory of Sion
protects the source of God's power on earth.

SOPHIE

Merde!

Sophie hits the breaks, lurching them both forward.
A hundred yards ahead, the intersection is blocked by
two DCPJ cars.

SOPHIE

All these things you know. You know
something about what happened to
him. Even if you don't know what.

Behind them, a fender bender. Angry SHOUTS of two
DRIVERS emerging from cars in the background.

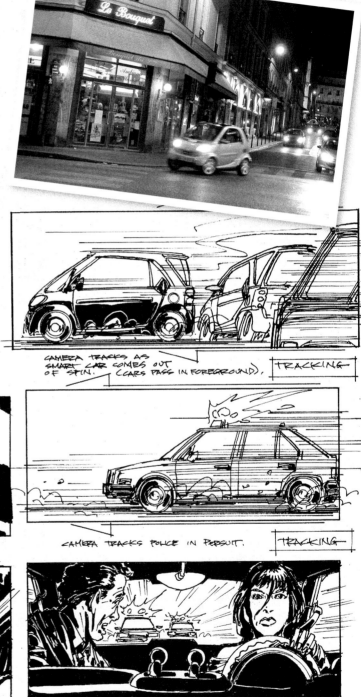

SOPHIE PULLS THE HANDBRAKE,

THEY SPIN,

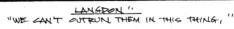

LANGDON
"WE CAN'T OUTRUN THEM IN THIS THING,"

Storyboards by Robert Ballantyne.

SOPHIE
That's why he wanted us to meet.

Bubble lights flash on. Two police cruisers start towards the commotion.

LANGDON
I'm in enough trouble as it is.

SOPHIE
I can't do this by myself. Please.

Blue light reflects in her imploring eyes. An endless beat.

LANGDON
Look, even *if we could* somehow get out of here —

SOPHIE
Okay!

Sophie throws the car, SCREECHING, into reverse. SIRENS scream to life. Sophie tears out, cop cars in fast pursuit.

SOPHIE: "NO, BUT WE CAN OUT-MANEUVER THEM!"

A, SMARTCAR LAUNCHES OVER CURB,

SMART CAR ANGLES FOR THE SIDEWALK,

CAMERA MOUNTED ON CAR

B ... AND PASSES OVER CAMERA,

C, POLICE CARS FOLLOW,

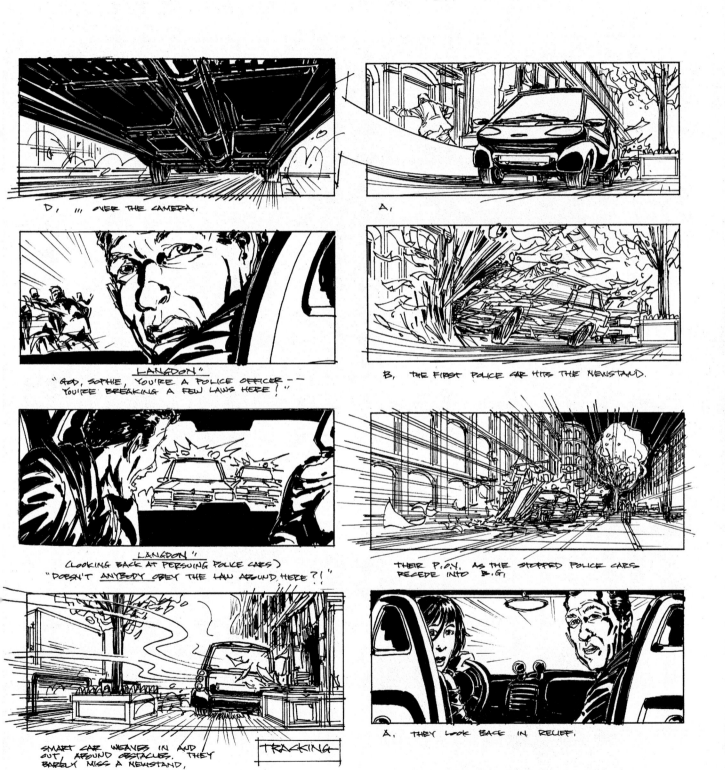

D, !!! OVER THE CAMERA.

A,

__LANGDON__"
"GOD, SOPHIE, YOU'RE A POLICE OFFICER ——
YOU'RE BREAKING A FEW LAWS HERE!"

B, THE FIRST POLICE CAR HITS THE NEWSTAND.

__LANGDON__"
(LOOKING BACK AT PERSUING POLICE CARS)
"DOESN'T ANYBODY OBEY THE LAW AROUND HERE?!"

THEIR P.O.V. AS THE STOPPED POLICE CARS
RECEDE INTO B.G.

SMART CAR WEAVES IN AND
OUT, AROUND OBSTACLES. THEY
BARELY MISS A NEWSTAND.

TRACKING

A, THEY LOOK BACK IN RELIEF.

Storyboards by Robert Ballantyne.

EXT. PARIS – CAR – MOVING
Sophie's smart car rips through the diplomatic quarter, the two squad cars not that far behind.

INT. SOPHIE'S CAR – MOVING – CONTINUOUS
Sophie is driving with impossible abandon. She takes a corner so hard, their seat belts are all that keep them in the car.

She is up on the sidewalk, barely missing a lamppost. Coming up on her right, a gap between two passing trucks.

> **LANGDON**
> You're not going to make it through that. No, no, no.

Sophie cuts the car hard right, impossibly squeaking through, turning back onto the thoroughfare of the Champs-Elysées. The police cars whip past in the other direction.

> **LANGDON**
> Okay. That was extraordinarily lucky.

She just shakes her head.

> **SOPHIE**
> We won't last long in this car. Fache doesn't like to be eluded. Even on a good day.

> **LANGDON**
> Right. Okay.

They're definitely both shaken.

> **SOPHIE**
> We need someplace to think.

Sophie has turned again.

> **SOPHIE**
> Do you have a credit card?

Ahead of them shines the glass roof of Nord train station.

EXT. NORD TRAIN STATION – NIGHT
A cop notices Sophie's smart car parked curbside. He activates his shoulder-mounted walkie-talkie.

A Very Smart Car

Rémy Julienne (a world-class French stunt coordinator) helped choreograph the reverse smart car chase through the streets of Paris. In order to safely navigate the oncoming vehicles, the body of a smart car was reversed. This allowed the car to appear as though it was being driven backward at high speed, when in fact the driver was facing forward in a normal position.

EXT. LOUVRE MUSEUM – NIGHT
Fache is in the face of the cop from the museum, the officer's back up hard against the exterior wall.

> **FACHE**
> **Why not just shoot the damn painting, you idiot?**

A cloud of smoke. Fache turns to find Collet, puffing a fresh stogie. Fache steps off, gesturing the scared cop away.

> **FACHE**
> **You should put it out in his eye.**

Collet inspects the cigar in his hand.

> **COLLET**
> **They found Neveu's car abandoned at the train station. Also two tickets to Brussels on Langdon's credit card.**

> **FACHE**
> **A decoy, I'm sure. Question all the taxi drivers. I'll put this on the wire.**

> **COLLET**
> **Interpol? Bezu, we have no definitive evidence he is guilty.**

> **FACHE**
> **I know he is guilty. Beyond doubt.**

Collet glances up, surprised.

> **FACHE**
> **Fugitives are most predictable in their first hour of flight. All share the same needs. Travel. Lodging. Cash. Stifle their access to these and they panic.**

A conviction here that is frightening.

> **FACHE**
> **A cryptographer and a school teacher? They will not last until dawn.**

EXT. PARIS – STREET – NIGHT – HIGH ANGLE
A taxi pulls curbside, near the edge of a sprawling park. Sophie and Langdon emerge as the cab pulls away.

> **LANGDON** (over)
> Bois de Boulogne.

EXT. BOIS DE BOULOGNE – NIGHT
Sophie and Langdon enter the park of lush green shadows.

> **SOPHIE**
> The mantis stays off the ant-hill, yes?

Resolving in the shadows, men, women, all available. Some slip away towards the street in pairs. Others satisfy their urges right there under cover of darkness.

LANGDON
Your police don't patrol this park.

They are approaching a stone wall where a JUNKIE sits cooking his works. Sophie reaches forward, pinches out his flame.

Langdon is startled, but no more so than the junkie, who stares up at her now with angry, feral eyes.

SOPHIE
Police Judiciaire.

This guy's clearly a predator. He could give a damn. But Sophie has actually reached out and touched his hand.

SOPHIE
500 francs for that. Come on. Go get a good meal instead.

Something in her TONE. The beat lasts. Then the man takes the cash from her other hand, going, leaving his fixings behind.

LANGDON
Did it ever occur to you that might be dangerous?

SOPHIE
No.

Simple as that.

LANGDON
He'll just use it to buy more.

Sophie is crushing the needle on the stone.

SOPHIE
Of course. Or maybe he'll eat. And
now we have a place to sit.

As they sit, Langdon turns the pendant over in his hand.

LANGDON
You could just have handed me a piece
of a UFO from Area 51.

SOPHIE
So, what does it have to do with his murder?

LANGDON
I have absolutely no idea.

SOPHIE
Come on, it means something.

LANGDON
No, no, no. It means lots of things.

SOPHIE
What's the next step? With him, it's
always "Sophie, what's the next step?"

That's when Langdon gets it. Lands hard.

LANGDON
A treasure hunt.

Sophie looks up at him. The beat lasts.

SOPHIE
To find his killer.

Sophie shakes her head.

SOPHIE
Maybe there is something about this
Priory of Sion.

LANGDON
I hope not. Any Priory story ends with
blood and death. They were butchered
by the Church.

Langdon looks into the forest beyond.

LANGDON
Going back to 1099, over a thousand
years ago, a king, a French king named
de Bouillon conquered Jerusalem.

*As Langdon speaks, armies race across the meadow
before him towards the low structures of ancient
Jerusalem beyond.*

LANGDON
Supposedly the invasion was to locate
an artifact lost since the time of Christ.
An artifact, it was said, the Church
would kill for.

*A king stands at meadow's edge with a group of men
around a giant table which is embossed with a giant
fleur-de-lis.*

LANGDON
To recover it, Bouillon founded a secret
brotherhood, the Priory of Sion, and their
military arm, the Knights Templar.

SOPHIE
But the Templars were created to protect
the Holy Land.

Historical Flashbacks

Dan Brown's novel relies heavily on the dynamic interaction between past and present. Ron Howard and Todd Hallowell, executive producer/2nd unit director, shot immense sequences that appear as historical flashbacks in the film to provide context and resonance for the contemporary story.

OPPOSITE and ABOVE: Production illustrations used to visualize the historical scenes. LEFT and RIGHT: Film stills of the historical flashbacks.

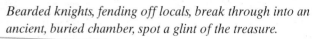

Bearded knights, fending off locals, break through into an ancient, buried chamber, spot a glint of the treasure.

LANGDON
According to this myth, that was a cover, to hide their true goal.

SOPHIE
And did they find it, this mysterious buried treasure?

Langdon can't help but smile at her skepticism.

LANGDON
Put it this way. One day, the Templars simply stopped searching, quit the Holy Land, and traveled directly to Rome.

In the meadow, nine bearded knights, square crosses on their chain-mail, face a tiny Pope in a silent standoff.

LANGDON
Whether they blackmailed the papacy or the Church bought their silence, no one knows.

Finally, it is the Pope who kneels. The Pope and his environs begin to morph forward in time.

LANGDON
But it is a fact that the papacy declared the Knights Templar of limitless power, independent of all kings and prelates, religious and political.

In the church, another Pope turns to face fifty messengers, handing out envelopes embossed with the papal seal.

LANGDON
This lasted until the 1300s, when the Church used their influence to effect a

stunning military maneuver. Sealed orders were issued all across Europe to be opened simultaneously. No easy task.

A soldier stands alone, opens the envelope in dawn's colors. Horsemen race across the horizon.

LANGDON
These orders stated God himself had shown Pope Clement V that the

Templars were devil worshipers, homosexuals and sodomites to boot.

A Templar knight is slaughtered in bed.

LANGDON
God had charged him with cleansing the earth of these heretics.

All over the meadow, Knights of Templar are captured, tortured, burned at the stake by the Vatican's soldiers.

LANGDON
The plan went off like clockwork. The knights were all but obliterated. It was October 13, 1307. A Friday.

SOPHIE
Friday the thirteenth.

Storyboards by Christopher Glass.

SOPHIE
Come on. Sauniere thought he knew the location of the Holy Grail?

LANGDON
Maybe more than that. This cross-and-flower looks ancient, but the metal under here is much newer.

He holds up the pendant.

LANGDON
There's a modern ID stamp: *24 Haxo*. And these tiny dots, they're read by a laser.

Hard not to see the fascination in his eyes.

LANGDON
This isn't just a pendant. It's a key.

She takes it, begins an inspection in moonlight.

LANGDON
There's no empirical evidence of the Priory, okay? Or of a Grail object. But if this key your grandfather left you —

SOPHIE
He left *us*, Professor.

She looks up at him now, offering up the key in her palm.

SOPHIE
And *vingt-quatre Haxo* is not an ID stamp. It's a street address.

INT. CASTLE GANDOLFO – NIGHT
RED WINE swirls like blood. Aringarosa takes a sip. Prefect ENTERS followed by three MEN, each older than the one before.

LANGDON
Now, was the Pope's true goal to steal the Templars' secret? If so, the artifact had already been surrendered to their masters, the Priory of Sion, and secreted away to destinations unknown.

Soldiers burst into that ancient, buried chamber, now empty save for the outline of a sarcophagus in the dirt floor.

SOPHIE
What artifact? The source of God's power on earth? I have never heard of any of this.

LANGDON
No, you have. Almost everyone on earth has. You just know it as the Holy Grail.

Sophie just stares at him.

A Key to the Code

This key, left behind by Sauniere, represents the first major discovery in Langdon and Sophie's journey. Featuring a fleur-de-lis within a Templar cross, the prop was specially made in Hong Kong, crafted in solid gold, platinum, and steel.

Aringarosa stands and bows. The three men bow. The newcomers take seats around the other end of the table.

PREFECT
Welcome, Bishop. This Council is convened.

All the other men and Aringarosa RESPOND as one.

OTHER MEN
In the name of the Father, the Son, and the Holy Ghost.

PREFECT
What business, say you?

A formality to his tone.

ARINGAROSA
You know of my request for funds —

YOUNG MAN
20 million euros in Papal Bearer Bonds. A tad more than petty cash, wouldn't you say, Bishop?

No love lost here.

ARINGAROSA
The endeavor is complex. And free-
dom has a great cost.

YOUNG MAN
And you will deliver us.

His tone is so without affect, you might miss the
contempt.

ARINGAROSA
I offer only a route to the renewal of
faith for all men.

YOUNG MAN
How humble —

PREFECT
Were we to grant your request, when
would this mission commence?

Aringarosa leans back in his chair, swirls his wine.

ARINGAROSA
Actually, tonight. It's already begun.
I do not presume. I act. This Vatican's
softening of Church law is impious and
cowardly. How much blood is spilled
every day because True Christian
Values lie in ruin?

He throws wine from his glass onto the old
wooden table.

ARINGAROSA
No more. Tonight the Grail will be
secured. Tonight the throne of Christ
will be sanctified.

He stares at them all, fire in his eyes.

ARINGAROSA
I was contacted by a man who called himself only the Teacher. He knew much about
this Council. And about the Priory . . .

INT. DCPJ HEADQUARTERS – NIGHT
Fache walks amid high-tech situation boards. A bustle of
activity. They could find your dog. A cop signals Fache.

FACHE
(activates speaker phone)
Fache.

COLLET *(on speaker)*
**Two hits. A taxi driver dropped them
in the 16th.**

EXT. RUE DE HAXO – NIGHT
Taxi WIPES to REVEAL Sophie and Langdon walking
into a courtyard past a sign: DEPOSITORY BANK OF
ZURICH.

SOPHIE
Mysterious. And annoying. Even in death.

Langdon inspects the key, and the key-sized slot in the wall.

LANGDON
Actually, I don't think he liked me very much.

Langdon inserts the pendant in the slot.
(OVER) A low HUM.

LANGDON
He made a joke once at my expense.
Got a pretty good laugh out of it.

COLLET *(over)*
We're close.

SOPHIE
Follow his clues. Like I am a girl again.

Langdon simply shrugs. Sophie inspects Langdon.

SOPHIE
Because of your expertise?

LANGDON
I'm sorry?

SOPHIE
About the Priory. Do you think that is why Sauniere sought you out? That he wanted us to meet?

LANGDON
Hell, I can name dozens of scholars who know a lot more about it.

They have come to a gunmetal door.

SOPHIE
What was it?

But the door swings inward, spilling bright white light.

INT. DEPOSITORY BANK OF ZURICH – NIGHT
Sophie and Langdon ENTER, their eyes wide. Illuminated grey metal everywhere. Floors, walls, even the lobby chairs.

GUARD
Bonsoir. **How may I help you?**

Unfazed by the hour, the armed GUARD at reception smiles. Langdon simply holds up the pendant.

GUARD
Of course. Rear door, please.

The guard watches Sophie and Langdon cross the lobby and disappear inside the single door set into the wall.

The guard glances down to his console. Amid security screens, a monitor shows scrolling thumbnail photos.

13/3. X. 21. 1-1-3-5
1.1 -2
1.1 2 - 3
1 1 2 3 = 5
1 1 2 3 5 = 8
1 1 2 3 5 5 + 9 13
1 1 2 3 5 3 +13 = 21
1 1 2 3 5 3 .13 21

FIBONACCI

24 Haxo: The Bank Set

Twenty-four rue Haxo doesn't actually exist in Paris. A real courtyard was selected because of its handsome, turn-of-the-century French exterior, but the goal was to create an interior (on a soundstage) that was surprisingly modern and high-tech.

BANQUE ZURICHOISE DE DEPOT

BANQUE
24
ZURICHOISE
DE DEPOT

The guard mouse-clicks and Langdon and Sophie's photos expand under the flashing word RECHERCHES and the Interpol logo.

The guard lifts a phone.

INT. DEPOSITORY BANK OF ZURICH – VIEWING ROOM
Sophie and Langdon step into another world. Oriental carpets and oak furniture. A MAN in a couture silk suit waits.

> **MAN (VERNET)**
> *Bonsoir.* **I am Andre Vernet, night manager.**

He smiles. Sophie and Langdon can only stare.

> **VERNET**
> **I take it this is your first visit to our establishment?**

Sophie glances at Langdon.

> **SOPHIE**
> Yes.

> **VERNET**
> Understood. Keys are often passed on and first-time users are sometimes uncertain of protocol.

> **LANGDON**
> Passed on?

> **VERNET**
> An inheritance.

Langdon glances at Sophie.

> **VERNET**
> Keys are essentially numbered Swiss accounts, often willed through generations. The shortest safety deposit box lease is fifty years.

> **SOPHIE**
> What's your longest account?

> **VERNET**
> Quite a bit longer. Technologies change. Keys are updated. But our accounts date back to the beginning of banking itself.

Langdon shoots Sophie a look.

> **LANGDON**
> The Templars invented banking.

> **VERNET**
> So they did.

Vernet leads them to a podium. A wide conveyor belt beyond enters the room in a graceful curve.

> **VERNET**
> Once the computer confirms your key,

enter your account number and your
box is retrieved.

Vernet gestures to a red switch on the wall.

                    VERNET
Should you require assistance. The
room is yours as long as you like.

                    SOPHIE
What if I lost track of my account
number? How might I recover it?

Again, that imperturbable smile.

                    VERNET
I'm afraid each key is paired with a ten-digit
number known only to the account bearer.

                    LANGDON
Employees do not have keys to the safe.

                    VERNET
Something like that. I hope you man-
age to remember it. A single wrong
entry disables the system.

And with a final smile, Vernet EXITS a side door.

                    SOPHIE
Ten.

Langdon nods, already in his pocket, pulls out a
familiar, once-crumpled page of numbers and lays it
on the podium.

                    LANGDON
Ten. Top of the sequence. Unscrambled
or scrambled?

                    SOPHIE
Unscrambled?

Langdon hands her the key.

                    LANGDON
It's yours, after all.

Sophie turns the key over in her hand.

                    SOPHIE
Funny. I don't even like history.

She slips it into the slot.

                    SOPHIE
I've never seen much good come from
looking to the past.

A sadness here, ever closer to the surface as she types in
the Fibonacci numbers from the sheet of paper.

                    LANGDON
Moment of truth.

Sophie hits the ENTER key. The screen blanks. A beat.
Then the conveyor belt begins to move. Sophie grins.

                    SOPHIE
I feel quite proud of myself considering I just did nothing.

                    LANGDON
Hell. Congratulations, then.

The box that coasts to a stop is large, industrial, with
metal clasps and bar code. Like a giant toolbox.

Sophie flips the clasps, opens the lid, and lifts out the
crate's sole contents. She hands it to Langdon.

VERNET
My guard alerted me to your status when you arrived. Yours is one of our oldest and highest-level accounts. Our bank prides itself on discretion. Your account includes a safe passage clause.

LANGDON
A what?

VERNET
I am obliged to assist you in safely departing the premises.

Vernet opens a door marked LOADING to reveal a windowless box the size of a very small room. He gestures.

VERNET
If you would step inside, please. Time is of the essence.

Langdon peers into the waiting space. So small. So dark. Sophie takes a beat, steps in. Langdon has gone pale.

LANGDON
In there?

BOX–CLOSE. Old, chipped wood. Ornate hinges. And on its surface, elegantly engraved, a single red rose.

That's when the side door opens again. Langdon quickly slips the box into his pocket as Vernet ENTERS.

VERNET
Forgive the intrusion. I'm afraid the police arrived more quickly than I anticipated.

Vernet is gesturing to the open side door.

VERNET
You must follow me, please. For your own safety.

INT. DEPOSITORY BANK OF ZURICH – CORRIDOR – WALKING
Langdon and Sophie trail Vernet down the gunmetal hall.

SOPHIE
You knew they were coming?

EXT. DEPOSITORY BANK OF ZURICH – NIGHT
Police cars surround the front of the building, bubble lights flashing. An armored truck lumbers up the exit ramp.

Collet steps into the truck's path, raising a flashing police badge. The driver stops, opens the door, leans out. Vernet, wearing a uniform.

> **VERNET**
> **Is there a problem?**

> **COLLET**
> **Police Judiciaire. I'm looking for two criminals.**

> **VERNET**
> **You came to the right place. They're all criminals here.**

Vernet's transformation is extraordinary. Demeanor, ACCENT, all are now perfectly working-class.

INT. ARMORED TRUCK – CONTINUOUS
Sophie sits on a narrow bench for one. Langdon sits on the floor beside her as the light goes off in this window-less hold.

> **COLLET** (over)
> **Open the hold.**

> **VERNET** (over)
> **Please. You think they trust us, the wages I get paid?**

Langdon is staring down, anxious, sweat beading on his temples, unaware he is nervously TAPPING the metal bench. Wordlessly, Sophie stills his hand with hers.

> **COLLET** (over)
> **You don't have keys to your own truck?**

EXT. DEPOSITORY BANK OF ZURICH – CONTINUOUS
Vernet hands back photos of Sophie and Langdon.

> **VERNET**
> **It's armored. Keys get sent to the destination. You mind? I'm on a schedule.**

> **COLLET**
> **Do all the drivers wear Rolexes?**

Vernet glances down, his watch peeking through his sleeve.

VERNET
This piece of shit? 40 euros in Barbès.

Vernet's smile grows bright with avarice.

VERNET
Yours for 35, eh?

In the background, another truck is stopped. A COP SHOUTS for Collet. Collet starts off.

VERNET
30 . . . Come on. 25 . . .

COLLET
Move along!

INT. CASTLE GANDOLFO – ITALY – NIGHT
Aringarosa and the Prefect now sit alone around the large table.

PREFECT
That was quite a performance.

ARINGAROSA
Little shit should know better than to play politics with me.

The Prefect says nothing.

ARINGAROSA
I know I got in front of you, old friend. I did as I thought best.

PREFECT
So, now what?

Aringarosa lifts his cell phone in his hand.

ARINGAROSA
Now we wait for the Teacher's call.

INT. ARMORED TRUCK – CARGO HOLD – MOVING
A single bulb flickers on, illuminating Langdon and Sophie in the small RUMBLING space. Sophie holds the box.

SOPHIE
The Holy Grail? You would think it would be bigger.

Langdon manages a wan smile. Sweat beads on his temples.

SOPHIE
A magic cup? The source of God's power on earth? It's nonsense.

LANGDON
You don't believe in God?

SOPHIE
No. I don't believe in some magic from the sky. Just people. And sometimes, that they can be kind.

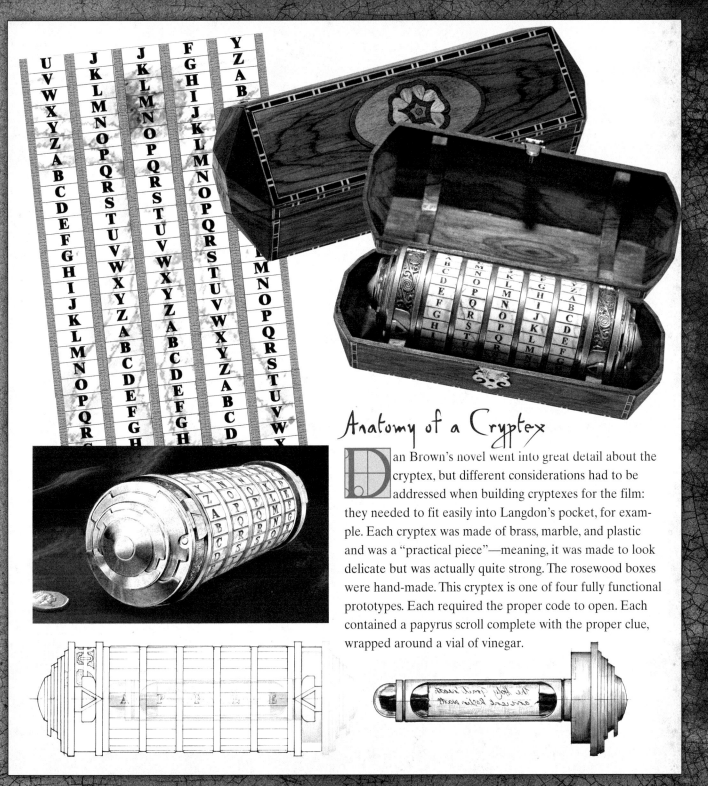

Anatomy of a Cryptex

Dan Brown's novel went into great detail about the cryptex, but different considerations had to be addressed when building cryptexes for the film: they needed to fit easily into Langdon's pocket, for example. Each cryptex was made of brass, marble, and plastic and was a "practical piece"—meaning, it was made to look delicate but was actually quite strong. The rosewood boxes were hand-made. This cryptex is one of four fully functional prototypes. Each required the proper code to open. Each contained a papyrus scroll complete with the proper clue, wrapped around a vial of vinegar.

LANGDON

That's enough?

SOPHIE

I think it has to be. I think it's all we have.

Not even a hint of sadness in her TONE.

SOPHIE

Are you a God-fearing man, Professor?

LANGDON

I was raised Catholic.

SOPHIE

That's not really an answer.

Sophie can't ignore the sweat on his face, his shaking hands.

SOPHIE

Professor, are you okay?

A tight shake of his head banishes the discussion.

LANGDON

Open it up.

Sophie stares at him, concerned.

LANGDON

Go on.

Sophie touches the engraved rose. She raises the top.

SOPHIE

This one is very old.

Sophie lifts a small cylinder from the padded interior. Stacked marble disks are embossed with letters in a brass framework sealed by a brass cap at each end.

SOPHIE

A cryptex. They're used to keep secrets.

In Sophie's hands, the cylinder's marble grows transparent, revealing the rolled parchment within.

SOPHIE

You write the information on a papyrus scroll which is then rolled around a thin glass vial.

Through the transparent marble, the parchment then becomes transparent itself, rolled around a glass vial.

SOPHIE

Of vinegar.

Through the transparent works, liquid sloshes in the vial.

SOPHIE

If you force it open, the vial breaks, vinegar dissolves papyrus, and your secret is lost forever.

The transparent vial of vinegar breaks and the transparent paper roll around it melts into meaningless pulp.

> SOPHIE
> The only way to access the information is to spell out the password with these.

The cryptex reconstitutes in Sophie's hand.

> SOPHIE
> Five dials, each with twenty-six letters, that's . . . twelve million possibilities.

> LANGDON
> I've never met a girl who knows that much about a cryptex.

Sophie flushes. Unexpected.

FLASH MATCH CUT past Sauniere's hands to little Sophie, wide eyed, as she opens a crude cryptex.

> SOPHIE
> Sauniere made one for me once.

> LANGDON
> My grandpa gave me a wagon.

> SOPHIE
> This clearly isn't the Holy Grail. Robert, what's going on?

The truck turns sharply. (OVER) A BANG as it hits a bump. Langdon just shuts his eyes, his entire body shaking.

> SOPHIE
> Please. You are not alright.

His finds a meager LAUGH.

> LANGDON
> I don't like small spaces.

> SOPHIE
> May I try something? I don't know why it works. My mother used to do it when I was scared, I think.

Sophie reaches out, takes his temples between her palms, presses her forehead to his, rocking slightly.

> LANGDON
> You think?

> SOPHIE
> My parents died in a car crash. With my brother. I was four.

INT. CAR – BACKSEAT – MOVING – NIGHT – FLASH CUT
Little Sophie sits amid coloring books as MOTHER turns to face her, soothingly massaging the child's temples.

> MOTHER
> **Mommy will make it better.**

The world EXPLODES behind mother's smile, glass flying.

EXT. HIGHWAY – NIGHT – FLASH CUT
Sauniere carries little Sophie away from the wreck of her parents' car, three body bags illuminated by bubble lights.

INT. ARMORED TRUCK – CARGO HOLD – MOVING
Sophie continues her slow, steady rocking.

> LANGDON
> I'm sorry.

> SOPHIE
> It was many years ago.

Finally she lets go as the truck turns off the road.

> SOPHIE
> Better?

> LANGDON
> Yes.
> *(surprised)*
> What did you do?

Faces close. Impossible to deny their proximity. (OVER) A BANG as the truck jumps from the silence of the highway.

> SOPHIE
> We're stopping.

Langdon slips the cryptex back into box and pocket. The rear door swings open to the cool night to reveal Vernet.

> VERNET
> Sorry about this.

He's holding a gun.

EXT. ROADSIDE – NIGHT – SAME MOMENT
The truck sits on a deserted stretch of dirt, the road visible in the distance under the pale moon.

> VERNET
> Bring it to me.

> LANGDON
> I don't have any idea what you're talking about.

Vernet simply shakes his head.

> VERNET
> Twenty years waiting for someone to come for that box and now it's you two murderers.

Vernet COCKS the hammer.

> VERNET
> Bring it to me.

Storyboards by Robert Ballantyne.

LANGDON

Listen, pal —

BANG! Vernet fires a bullet into the wall above Langdon's head, spent shell CLINKING to the cargo hold floor.

LANGDON
(freaked)

Okay! Okay!

VERNET

Right. Now.

INT. ARMORED TRUCK – CARGO HOLD – NIGHT – CONTINUOUS

Langdon reaches into his pocket, removes the box. He steps towards the open truck door. Vernet retreats a pace.

VERNET

Place it near the edge of the door.

Langdon kneels, deposits the box at the edge of the hold.

VERNET

Stand up.

VERNET:
"STEP AWAY FROM THE BOX,"
(LANGDON STEPS BACK,),

VERNET GRABS BOX AND STARTS TO CLOSE DOORS,
VERNET:
"I WISH YOU LUCK WITH THE POLICE, OF COURSE,"

A,
VERNET:
"RETURN TO THE BACK WALL AND TURN AROUND, YOU TOO, MADEMOISELLE,"

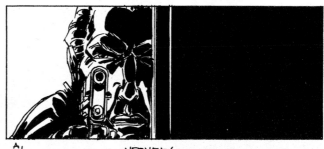

A,
VERNET:
"ALTHOUGH I CANNOT IMAGINE THE TALE OF WOE OF THOSE ON A KILLING SPREE,,,"

B,

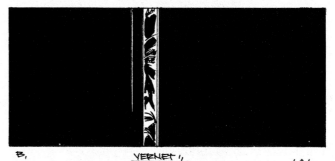

B,
VERNET:,
",,, WILL HOLD MUCH WATER,"
(THE HOLD GOES DARK,),

Langdon obliges, clocking the spent pistol shell.

>   **VERNET**
> Step away from the box. No one will lose
> sleep over a couple on a killing spree.

Langdon discreetly brushes the spent shell with his foot
into the lower frame of the door's crafted sill.

>   **VERNET**
> Return to the back wall and turn
> around. You too, mademoiselle.

Sophie and Langdon do as they are told and Vernet grabs
the box, SLAMMING the truck door TO BLACK.

EXT. ARMORED TRUCK – ROADSIDE – SAME MOMENT
Vernet reaches up to slide the exterior latch. But the
door has stopped just short of fitting into the sill.

Vernet shoves hard. An unexpected CRUNCH but the
door still doesn't close. He throws his shoulder against it.

The door explodes outward, SMASHING Vernet in the face,
SHATTERING his nose and sending him reeling backward.

C.U. — TIRES SPIN AND RACE OUT OF FRAME.

A. TRUCK RACES AWAY.

B. CAMERA DOLLIES BACK — PAST VERNET
AS HE SHOOTS AT THE TRUCK.

DOLLY BACK

A. C.U. OF TRUCK MUFFLER — IT'S
HIT BY A BULLET AND DRAGS ON
THE ROAD — SHOOTING OFF A TRAIL
OF SPARKS BEHIND IT.

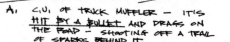

TRACKING

Langdon hits the gravel, cutting his hand, grabbing the box as Vernet falls. Vernet stares past the now crushed shell as Sophie races for the passenger's side door.

Vernet vomits into his own blood, scrambles to his gun. The truck, muffler almost dislodging, jumps back onto the road.

Vernet manages to get off a few SHOTS but they go wide as the truck pulls away into the night.

INT. CASTLE GANDOLFO – ITALY – STAIRWAY – NIGHT
Murals adorn high walls. Aringarosa and the Prefect climb steep steps.

> **PREFECT**
> You have put tremendous faith in this teacher of yours.

> **ARINGAROSA**
> Yes. And no. I have another pair of eyes he does not know of.

> **PREFECT**
> Sound policy, always.

> **ARINGAROSA**
> And I have given him an angel to do his will. For surely God has no better soldier than my Silas.

> **PREFECT**
> That monk of yours. Devotion is one thing —

(OVER) Aringarosa's cell phone RINGS.

Storyboards by Robert Ballantyne.

ARINGAROSA

Aringarosa . . . No.

His expression goes dark. He locks eyes with the Prefect.

ARINGAROSA

The keystone is lost.

EXT. ARMORED TRUCK – HIGH ANGLE

GLIDE over fields cut by a single road. FIND an armored truck, Sophie's head out her open door, hair whipping.

INT. ARMORED TRUCK – CONTINUOUS

Sophie pulls her head back in. Skin flushed, windswept. (OVER) The DRAGGING muffler protests rhythmically.

LANGDON

Better?

SOPHIE

Always, if I got too nervous, I had to put my head out of the window not to be sick.

Her breath is short, eyes agitated. Langdon tamps the blood from his palm with tissues from a box on the dashboard.

SOPHIE

Sauniere used to say I was like a dog.
(*off his look*)
A cute dog. A little dog.

She opens the box. Two desperate confused souls.

SOPHIE

And somebody murders him.
Somebody shoots at us. For this.

Sophie has lifted the cryptex, begun turning the dials.

LANGDON

What happened between you and your grandfather, Sophie?

Sophie turns to him, surprised.

LANGDON

My shoulder hurts. I've been shot at.
Be straight with me.

She just shakes her head. Langdon is pulling puzzle pieces out of the air, trying to make some sense out of all this.

LANGDON

You say he raised you, but you two don't talk anymore. You call him by his last name.

Sophie has formed G – R – A – I – L on the cryptex. It does not open.

LANGDON

You say you hate history. Nobody hates history, they hate their own histories.

SOPHIE

Now you are a psychologist, too?

Sophie forms the word: V – I – N – C – I. No luck.

LANGDON

What if Sauniere was starting to groom you?

SOPHIE

What do you mean, groom me?

Sophie is finishing another word, S – O – F – I – A. Nothing.

LANGDON

In secret societies, kids are trained
from an early age to understand codes
and symbols, to keep secrets.

(OVER) Sophie hears a familiar SLAP, her own
younger SCREAM.

LANGDON

Your grandfather gave you puzzles
and cryptexes as a child. Say, Sauniere
hopes you will one day join him in
the Priory.

He's got that look again, wheels turning, very fast.

LANGDON

Whatever interrupts your relationship
abrogates that process. But years later
he imagines the Grail is in danger, so
he reaches out to you.

SOPHIE

Now I'm being groomed by Santa
Claus? So you're saying all this is real.
The Priory. The Holy Grail?

LANGDON

We've been dragged into a world of
people who think this stuff is real. Real
enough to kill for.

SOPHIE

Who?

LANGDON

I'm out of my field here.

The moment lasts forever, the two sitting in silence.
Neither one has any idea what to do next. Finally . . .

LANGDON

I know a Grail historian. Absolutely
obsessed with Priory myth. An
Englishman but he lives here in
France. At Château Villette.

SOPHIE

Le Château de la Villette? In Versailles?

LANGDON

Yes, that's the one.

SOPHIE

Ah, nice friends.

Langdon shrugs. He glances at the dashboard.

LANGDON

Damn, we're almost empty.

Sophie leans over to the bottomed-out gas gauge.
Flicks it with her finger twice, hard. It springs up
to nearly full.

SOPHIE

Not French engineering.

She looks out at the night.

SOPHIE

Do you trust this man? Fache could
even be offering a reward.

Langdon shrugs.

LANGDON

One thing Sir Leigh doesn't need is money.

SOPHIE

Sir Leigh?

LANGDON
We're on a Grail quest, Sophie. Who better to help us than a knight?

INT. FRENCH HOSPITAL – TRIAGE – NIGHT
Vernet sits on a gurney, head shaved and stitched. The curtain slides open and Fache ENTERS.

FACHE
According to your records, it seems you are not a driver after all.

Vernet says nothing, simply stares up at him.

FACHE
And that you have lost your tongue along with your truck.

Fache's smile is all business.

FACHE
Aiding and abetting two murder suspects. This carries jail time.

VERNET
Please speak with my lawyers.

FACHE
I could do that, yes. But all this confusion. Violence. Vanishing property. While I did so, it might get around that your bank's services were less than ideal.

The moment lasts.

VERNET
What do you want?

FACHE
Your trucks carry transponders. I want that homing device activated. Right now.

The two stare at each other. Then Vernet looks down.

VERNET
As you wish.

EXT. CHATEAU VILLETTE – ESTABLISHING SHOTS
185 acres of forests and gardens; two flat rectangular lakes; a house more castle than mansion.

VOICE (REMY) (over)
My master is asleep. Come back tomorrow.

FIND a familiar armored truck, stopped at the front gate.

LANGDON (over)
Tell him it's a matter of life and death.

INT. ARMORED TRUCK – CHATEAU VILLETTE GATE – NIGHT
An imposing security gate. Langdon leans over Sophie, SPEAKING into the intercom outside her half-open door.

SOPHIE
It's on the wrong side.

LANGDON
He likes all things English. Including his cars.

INTERCOM (TEABING)
Robert, do I owe you money?

LANGDON
Leigh. Any chance you'll open up for an old friend?

INTERCOM (TEABING)
Of course.

Sophie's look says, That was easy. Langdon's head shake says, Just you wait.

INTERCOM (TEABING)
But first, a test of honor. Three questions.

LANGDON
Fire away.

INTERCOM (TEABING)
Your first: shall I serve coffee or tea?

LANGDON
Tea, of course.

INTERCOM (TEABING)
Excellent. Second, milk or lemon?

LANGDON
That would depend on the tea.

INTERCOM (TEABING)
Correct. And now the third and most grave
of inquiries. In which year did a Harvard
sculler out-row an Oxford man at Henley?

Langdon holds a moment, clueless. Then smiles.

LANGDON
Surely such a travesty has never occurred.

INTERCOM (TEABING)
Your heart is true. You may pass.

The gate CLICKS, slowly swinging open. They drive
forward, between low leaning trees towards the giant
house ahead.

LANGDON
Teabing's spent his life searching for
the Grail. So that thing is one hot *tamale*.

Her look to him: *tamale*?

LANGDON
Hot coal? Hot potato?

SOPHIE
So, you want to keep our chest close to
our cards, yes?

LANGDON
Very close. Yes.

Langdon has pulled the truck behind a thick hedge.

SOPHIE
I still don't know why he put you into
this. And I am sorry.

Langdon SHUTS off the ENGINE.

SOPHIE
But I am also very glad.

He's not sure what to say. She's already out her door.

EXT. CHATEAU VILLETTE – NIGHT – MOMENTS LATER
Before Langdon can knock, the door swings open. A
MAN (REMY) in pinstripe trousers and black jacket
ushers them in. HOLD on Remy a beat as he stares out
into the darkness.

INT. CHATEAU VILLETTE – FOYER – CONTINUOUS
An octagonal room looking over sprawling gardens and
floodlit waterfall outside the back windows.

REMY
You are requested to make yourself at home.

And with that, Remy EXITS.

VOICE *(over)*
Robert. And you travel with a maiden, it seems.

At the top of the giant staircase that curls up to the
second floor, a figure starts down from the shadows.

LANGDON
Sir Leigh Teabing. May I present
Sophie Neveu.

The figure moves into the light. Handsome. Perpetual
laughter in bright, sharp eyes. This is LEIGH TEABING.

TEABING
*Je vous présènte mes hommages, tardifs,
mais sincères.*

As Teabing descends the stairs, Sophie can see the metal
cane and brace he uses to aid his unwieldy legs.

SOPHIE
Thank you for having us. I realize it's
quite late.

TEABING
It's so late it's early, mademoiselle.

Teabing ENTERS and takes her hand, bowing low.

TEABING
What a lovely smile you have.

Sophie clocks a wedding picture on the mantel. Teabing,
so much younger, beside a beautiful girl with flowing
red hair.

TEABING
You both look quite shaken. Well, we
all know the remedy for that.

Teabing smiles.

> **TEABING**
> Earl Grey.

> **LANGDON**
> Lemon.

> **TEABING**
> Correct.

INT. DCPJ HEADQUARTERS – NIGHT
Fache stands in front of a wall-mounted electronic
map, a TECHNICIAN at a terminal in front of him.

> **TECHNICIAN**
> **Truck's signal coming on line —**

> **FACHE**
> **Just tell me when you have it!**

On screen, a shifting of maps. A cursor starts to flash.

> **TECHNICIAN**
> **Locked on and tracking, sir.**

Fache is already heading for the door.

> **FACHE**
> **Relay the location to Collet. He is not
> to move in until I arrive.**

FAVOR FACHE as he strides out the front door into . . .

EXT. DCPJ HQ – NIGHT
Streetlight spreads the color of butter. Fache climbs into
his car. Starts the engine.

INT. FACHE'S CAR – NIGHT
Fache takes a beat, checking to see if anyone is around.
The street is all but abandoned.

He clocks his Cross in the World in the rearview mirror.
Then Fache takes out his cell phone. Hits an autodial key.

INT. CASTLE GANDOLFO – BILLIARD ROOM – NIGHT
3, 2, 1, and 4 balls cluster on green felt and BREAK,
flying from the cue ball in all directions. TILT UP as
the Prefect watches Aringarosa anxiously answer his
RINGING cell phone.

INT. FACHE'S CAR – NIGHT
Fache WHISPERS into his phone.

> **FACHE**
> *Monseigneur.*

INT. CASTLE GANDOLFO – BILLIARD ROOM – NIGHT
Aringarosa listens, now nods with relief.

> **ARINGAROSA**
> Thank God.

INT. CHATEAU VILLETTE – KITCHEN – NIGHT
Sub-Zeros. Wolf ranges. Teabing and Langdon sit with
Sophie, who pulls back her hair in the reflective surface.

Remy serves bangers and mash and brown sauce along with the tea.

SOPHIE
Thank you. I can't.

TEABING
You must. Remy is from Lyon. Nevertheless he is fantastic with sauces.

Remy SNORTS, commences cleaning up. Langdon finishes washing his cut palm in the sink. All is British politesse, but the strangeness is lost on no one.

TEABING
A dramatic late-night arrival. Mention of life and death. What can an old cripple do for you, Robert?

LANGDON
We'd like to talk about the Priory of Sion.

Something changes in Teabing's eyes, a sudden sharpening —

TEABING
The keepers? The secret war? Impossible.

— and then it's gone; that playful light is back in his eyes.

TEABING
No, I simply cannot believe that Robert Langdon, Professor Robert Langdon, would want to know a single thing about such, what was the phrase, wing-nut nonsense.

Langdon winces. Their own history here.

LANGDON
Did I really say wing-nut? Okay, I haven't been particularly receptive to your ideas.

TEABING
I have never held your lack of imagination against you. But to arrive so late, with no explanation —

LANGDON
Leigh. Please. I'm sorry to be so mysterious. But I am into something here I can't understand.

TEABING
You? Really?

LANGDON
Not without your help.

Teabing holds his gaze a beat longer. Actually CLAPS.

Teabing's Walking Sticks

In the novel, Teabing uses crutches. For the movie, Ron Howard and Ian McKellen experimented with various walking aids and decided that the use of two canes would best fit the personality of the character (as well as the action required in the movie). These canes were all hand-designed, and featured a variety of symbols in keeping with Teabing's passions. At left, conceptual designs for the walking sticks; below, the final props used in the movie.

TEABING
Playing to my vanity. Robert. You should be ashamed.

Teabing is smiling, Langdon smiling back.

LANGDON
Not if it works.

TEABING
There are always four. The Grand Master and three *sénéchaux* make up the primary guardians of the Grail. But the Priory's members span our very globe itself.

LANGDON
Philippe de Cherisey exposed it as a hoax in 1967.

TEABING
That is what they want you to believe.

Langdon simply opens his hands.

TEABING
The Priory is charged with a single task. To protect the greatest secret in modern history.

SOPHIE
The source of God's power on earth. He told me this silliness already.

TEABING
Ah, a common misunderstanding. The Priory protects the source of the *Church's* power on earth. The Holy Grail.

SOPHIE
I don't understand. What power? Some magic dishes?

Teabing looks at her and smiles.

TEABING
Oh, Robert, I suppose you've been telling her the Holy Grail's a cup.
(*to Sophie*)
To understand the Grail you must first understand the Bible.

EXT. PARIS – BANK OF THE SEINE
Silas stares into the dark waters. If suicide were not a sin he'd be well under by now.

INT. CAR – PARKING LOT – FLASH CUT
Silas reaches over the front seat, breaks a MAN'S (40s) neck with strong arms, Paris out the windows behind him.

INT. GREENHOUSE – OUTSIDE PARIS – FLASH CUT
A MAN (50s) mists a sea of hydroponically grown moss. Silas rises and slits his throat, red spilling on green.

INT. APARTMENT – L'ILE SAINT-LOUIS – FLASH CUT
Notre Dame out the windows. Silas shoots a MAN (40s).

INT. LOUVRE – NIGHT – FLASH CUT
Sauniere falls back as Silas's bullet hits him.

EXT. PARIS – BANK OF THE SEINE

The water continues to beckon the monk. (OVER) A phone RINGS. Silas answers.

> **SILAS**
>
> *Sí.*
> *(eyes closing in relief)*
> *Sí.*

He is already gone, like smoke.

INT. CHATEAU VILLETTE – KITCHEN – NIGHT

Langdon and Sophie sit with Teabing, still eating.

> **TEABING**
>
> The Good Book did not arrive by fac-simile from heaven.

Sophie's look of mock disappointment makes Teabing grin.

> **TEABING**
>
> The Bible, as we know it, was finally presided over by one man. The pagan emperor Constantine.

> **SOPHIE**
>
> I thought Constantine was a Christian.

As Teabing speaks, the room behind him grows light, an old man lies in bed, a priest bent over him.

> **TEABING** *(over)*
>
> Hardly. He was a lifelong pagan who was baptized on his deathbed.

PUSH OUT ancient windows to see Rome, 325AD. A giant temple.

> **TEABING** *(over)*
>
> Constantine was Rome's supreme holy man. For centuries, his people had worshiped a balance between nature's male deities and the Goddess, or sacred feminine.

On the altar stands a priestess. Goddess statuary is everywhere. Pagans worship orgiastically.

> **TEABING** *(over)*
>
> But a growing religious turmoil was gripping Rome. Three centuries earlier

The Script Supervisor's Code

The script supervisor, Annie Penn, recorded highly detailed notes for every take of every scene that was shot, noting camera angles, gestures, prop placement, and every element that would be used to ensure continuity between takes during editing. Because scenes are frequently shot out of order, and from many different angles, the script supervisor's notes (right) become a crucial record of the shoot for the director.

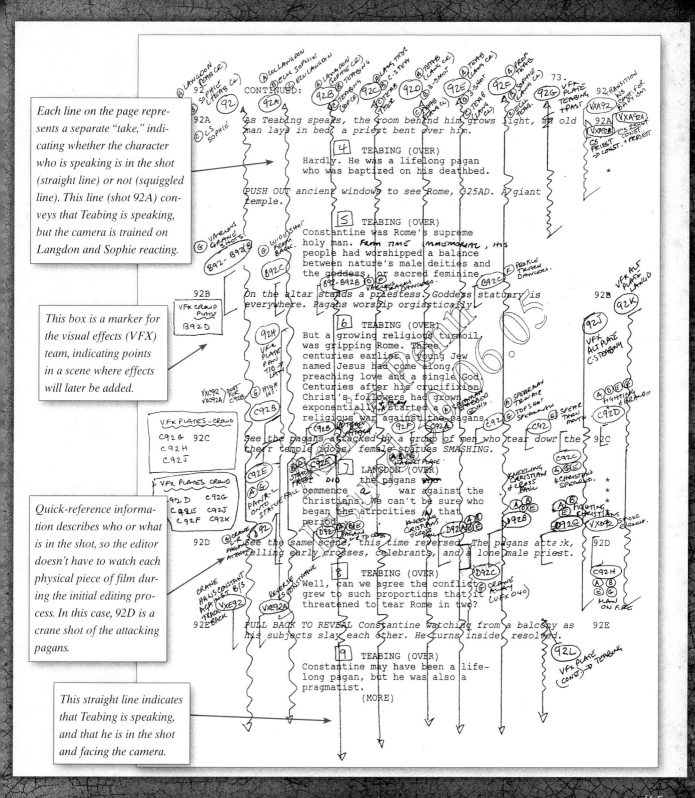

Each line on the page represents a separate "take," indicating whether the character who is speaking is in the shot (straight line) or not (squiggled line). This line (shot 92A) conveys that Teabing is speaking, but the camera is trained on Langdon and Sophie reacting.

This box is a marker for the visual effects (VFX) team, indicating points in a scene where effects will later be added.

Quick-reference information describes who or what is in the shot, so the editor doesn't have to watch each physical piece of film during the initial editing process. In this case, 92D is a crane shot of the attacking pagans.

This straight line indicates that Teabing is speaking, and that he is in the shot and facing the camera.

73.

CONTINUED:

As Teabing speaks, the room behind him grows light, an old man lays in bed, a priest bent over him.

4   TEABING (OVER)
Hardly. He was a lifelong pagan
who was baptized on his deathbed.

PUSH OUT ancient windows to see Rome, 325AD. A giant temple.

5   TEABING (OVER)
Constantine was Rome's supreme
holy man. From time immemorial, his
people had worshipped a balance
between nature's male deities and
the goddess, or sacred feminine.

On the altar stands a priestess. Goddess statuary is everywhere. Pagans worship orgiastically.

6   TEABING (OVER)
But a growing religious turmoil
was gripping Rome. Three
centuries earlier a young Jew
named Jesus had come along,
preaching love and a single God.
Centuries after his crucifixion
Christ's followers had grown
exponentially. Started a
religious war against the pagans.

See the pagans attacked by a group of men who tear down their temple idols, female statues SMASHING.

7   LANGDON (OVER)
Did the pagans commence a war against the
Christians. We can't be sure who
began the atrocities in that
period.

See the same scene, this time reversed. The pagans attack, felling early crosses, celebrants, and a lone male priest.

8   TEABING (OVER)
Well, can we agree the conflict
grew to such proportions that it
threatened to tear Rome in two?

PULL BACK TO REVEAL Constantine watching from a balcony as his subjects slay each other. He turns inside, resolved.

9   TEABING (OVER)
Constantine may have been a lifelong pagan, but he was also a
pragmatist.
(MORE)

115

a young Jew named Jesus had come along, preaching love and a single God. Centuries after his crucifixion, Christ's followers had grown exponentially, started a religious war against the pagans.

See the pagans attacked by a group of men who tear down the temple idols, female statues SMASHING.

LANGDON (*over*)
Or it was the pagans who commenced making war against the Christians. We can't be sure who began the atrocities of that period, Leigh.

See the same scene, this time reversed. The pagans attack, felling early crosses, celebrants, and a lone male priest.

TEABING (*over*)
Well, can we agree the conflict grew to such proportions that it threatened to tear Rome in two?

PULL BACK TO REVEAL Constantine watching from a balcony as his subjects slay each other. He turns inside, resolved.

TEABING (*over*)
Constantine may have been a lifelong pagan, but he was also a pragmatist. So in 325 Anno Domini he decided to unify Rome under a single religion. Christianity.

Sophie looks up at Langdon, startled. He nods.

LANGDON
Christianity was on the rise. He didn't want his empire torn apart.

TEABING
To strengthen the new Christian tradition, Constantine held a famous ecumenical gathering known as the Council of Nicaea.

In a cavernous room now behind Teabing, robed men including Constantine SHOUT at each other around a large stone table.

TEABING (*over*)
And at this council, the many sects of Christianity debated and voted on — everything from the acceptance and rejection of specific gospels to the date of Easter to the administration of sacraments.

Hands go up. One man stabs the table with a dagger.

TEABING (*over*)
And, of course, the mortality of Jesus.

SOPHIE
I don't follow.

TEABING
Ma chérie. Until that moment in history, Jesus was viewed by many of his followers as a mighty prophet, a great and powerful man, but a man nonetheless. A mortal man.

LANGDON
Some followers believed he was mortal. Some believed he was divine.

SOPHIE
Not the Son of God?

TEABING
Not even his nephew twice removed.

SOPHIE
Hold on. You're saying Jesus' divinity came from a vote?

TEABING
Remember, in those days gods were everywhere. By infusing Jesus The Man with divine magic, making him capable of earthly miracles and his own resurrection, Constantine turned him into a god *within* the human world. He basically knocked the more distant gods out of the game.

LANGDON
Constantine didn't create Jesus' divinity, Leigh. He simply sanctioned a widely held idea.

TEABING
Semantics.

LANGDON
No, it's not semantics. You're interpreting facts to support your own conclusions.

TEABING
Fact. For many Christians, Jesus was mortal one day and divine the next.

LANGDON
For a *few* Christians, Jesus had his divinity enhanced.

TEABING
Absurd. There was even a formal announcement of his promotion.

SOPHIE
Excuse me!

She has gotten both their attention.

SOPHIE
Who is God? Who is man?

She is looking right at Langdon.

SOPHIE
How many have been murdered over this question?

Teabing registers the word "murder" in an instant. Something moves across his eyes again. And again, he hides it.

TEABING
Exactly. As long as there has been The One True God, there has been killing in his name.

Sophie and Langdon exchange a look. Teabing is already using his cane to stand.

TEABING
Now let me show you the Grail.

Teabing's Slide Show

In order to better express Teabing's obsessive relationship with *The Last Supper*, the fresco appears on a high-tech video screen within Teabing's study in the movie. This allows Teabing to draw the viewer's eye to various details of the Da Vinci work.

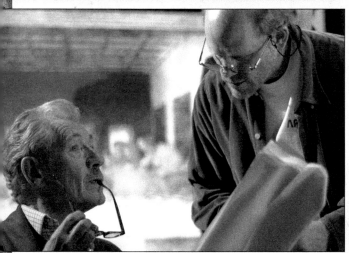

INT. AUDI – NIGHT – MOVING
Silas shoots down the highway, literally pushing the
engine to its limit, over 200 kph. See those eyes. Truly
possessed.

INT. CHATEAU VILLETTE – BALLROOM – NIGHT
Remy watches from the hall as Sophie and Langdon
follow Teabing through a maze of artifacts and hi-tech
equipment.

> **TEABING**
> This used to be the ballroom. I have
> little occasion to dance these days.

Pass blowups of the Sumerian Tablets and arrive at
an eight-foot monitor showing *The Last Supper* on
an easel.

> **TEABING**
> I trust you recognize Leonardo Da
> Vinci's fresco. Now, my dear, if you
> would close your eyes.

> **LANGDON**
> Leigh, save the parlor tricks?

> **TEABING**
> You asked for *my* help, I recall. Allow
> an old man his indulgences.

Sophie glances at Langdon, who nods. A beat. Sophie
obliges.

> **TEABING**
> Now, mademoiselle, where is Jesus sitting?

TEABING

No single cup. No chalice. A bit strange, don't you think, considering both the Bible and standard Grail legend celebrate this moment as the definitive arrival of the Holy Grail. Now, Robert, you can be of some help to us. Would you be so kind as to show us the symbols for man and woman, please?

LANGDON

No balloon animals? I do a great duck.

Langdon steeples his hands into a pyramid.

LANGDON

This is the original icon for male. A rudimentary phallus.

SOPHIE

In the middle.

SOPHIE

Quite to the point.

TEABING

Good. He and his disciples are breaking bread. And what drink?

TEABING

Yes, indeed.

SOPHIE

Wine. They drank wine.

TEABING

Splendid. Now a final question. How many wineglasses on the table?

SOPHIE

One? The Holy Grail?

TEABING

Open your eyes.

Sophie looks at the image. Everyone at the table has a cup. Including Christ.

LANGDON
Known as the Blade, it represents
aggression and manhood. The symbol
is still used today on modern military
uniforms.

TEABING
The more penises you have, the higher
the rank. Boys will be boys.

LANGDON
And, as you would imagine, the female
symbol is the exact opposite.

Langdon inverts the steeple, now an inverted pyramid.

LANGDON
This is called the Chalice.

TEABING
The Chalice resembles a cup, or vessel,
and, more importantly, the shape of a
woman's womb.

Teabing has made the same shape with his hands. Oddly,
it looks almost like both men are praying.

TEABING
No, the Grail has never been a cup.
The Grail is literally the ancient symbol for womanhood. In this case a
woman who carried a secret so powerful that, if revealed, it would devastate
the very foundations of Christianity.

SOPHIE
Wait, please. You're saying the Holy
Grail is a person? A woman?

TEABING
And it turns out she makes an appear-
ance here after all.

INT. CHATEAU VILLETTE – BALLROOM – NIGHT
Sophie stands close, inspecting the painting.

SOPHIE
But they're all men.

TEABING
Are they? How about the figure at the
right hand of the Lord? Seated in the
place of honor?

Teabing works a mouse. DETAILS of the painting
illuminate as he speaks, not simple reproduction but
a flat-screen render.

TEABING
Flowing red hair. Folded, feminine
hands. The hint of a bosom, no?

SOPHIE
Incroyable.

TEABING
Pas tout à fait. It's called scotoma. The
mind sees what it wants.

Langdon shakes his head. He can see where this is going.

LANGDON
Leigh, not this old chestnut.

SOPHIE
Who is she?

TEABING
My dear, that is Mary Magdalen.

SOPHIE
The prostitute?

TEABING
She was no such thing. Smeared by the Church in 591, poor dear. Mary Magdalen was Jesus' wife.

Langdon covers his eyes with his palm, head shaking.

EXT. CHATEAU VILLETTE – GROUNDS – NIGHT
A familiar black Audi cruises past the main gates.

INT. CHATEAU VILLETTE – BALLROOM
Langdon and Teabing are in mid, well . . . conversation.

LANGDON
It's an old wives' tale, Leigh —

TEABING
The original, in fact —

LANGDON
There's virtually no empirical proof —

TEABING
I needn't prove anything, Robert. I am not the one banging on doors at two in the morning, am I?

Landgon doesn't have a comeback.

TEABING
And you know as well as I do there is much evidence to support it.

Sophie turns to Langdon, who wants to deny it, just SIGHS.

LANGDON
Theories. There are theories.

TEABING
Notice how Jesus and Mary are clothed, mirror images of each other.

LANGDON
The mind sees what it expects. We find the meanings we want.

Teabing works the mouse. Jesus' red robe and Mary's red cloak illuminate. Then Jesus' blue cloak and Mary's blue robe.

TEABING
Venturing into the more bizarre, notice that Jesus and Mary appear to be joined at the hip and are leaning away from each other as if to create a shape in the negative space between them. Leonardo gives us the Chalice.

On the screen, that negative space illuminates, creating the indisputable inverted pyramid of the Chalice sign.

TEABING
And notice what happens if these two figures swap sides.

Mary slides over to lean on Jesus' shoulder, a perfect fit.

> **SOPHIE**
> Okay, but it is not exactly a photograph.

> **TEABING**
> No.

> **SOPHIE**
> Just because Da Vinci painted it does not make it true.

> **TEABING**
> No. But history, old sow, she does. Listen, now. The Gospel of Philip.

> **SOPHIE**
> Philip?

Langdon nods, not happy about it.

> **TEABING**
> Rejected at Nicaea along with any other gospels that made Jesus appear human and not divine.

Teabing has lifted a book, easily at hand. He reads.

EXT. CHATEAU VILLETTE – GROUNDS – NIGHT
On the edge of the expansive, moonlit grounds, Audi in the background, Silas runs straight for the tall wrought-iron fence.

> **TEABING** *(over)*
> *And the companion of the Savior is Mary Magdalen . . .*

He leaps, impossibly high, grabbing the tops of the bars and hoisting himself over.

> **TEABING** *(over)*
> *Christ loved her more than all the disciples. And used to kiss her on —*

INT. CHATEAU VILLETTE – BALLROOM – NIGHT
Sophie INTERRUPTS.

> **SOPHIE**
> This says nothing of marriage.

> **TEABING**
> Actually —
> *(to Sophie)*
> Robert?

Teabing shows both palms to Langdon. Enjoying this.

> **LANGDON**
> *(grudging)*
> Actually, in those days, the word "companion" literally meant spouse.

Teabing has opened another book, that laughter in the eyes twinkling ever brighter.

> **TEABING**
> And this is from the gospel of Mary Magdalen herself.

> **SOPHIE**
> She wrote a . . .

> **LANGDON**
> She may have.

> **TEABING**
> Robert. Fight fair.

> **LANGDON**
> She may have.

TEABING
(reading)
And Peter said . . . Did he prefer her to
us? And Levi answered, Peter . . .

EXT. CHATEAU VILLETTE – NIGHT
Silas races through the forest, cilice belt giving him a
wolf's lope.

TEABING *(over)*
I see you contending against the
woman like an adversary.

Silas closes on the house lights in the distance.

TEABING *(over)*
If the Savior made her worthy, who are
you indeed to reject her?

INT. CHATEAU VILLETTE – BALLROOM – NIGHT
Teabing sets down the book.

TEABING
Jesus tells Mary Magdalen it is up to
her to continue his church.

Teabing highlights Peter leaning menacingly toward
Mary Magdalen, an angry crowd behind him.

TEABING
Mary Magdalen. Not Peter. The church was
supposed to be carried on by a woman.

See Peter as he slices a blade-like hand across her neck.

TEABING
Few realize Magdalen was a powerful
woman in her own right.

SOPHIE

She was?

LANGDON

Mary Magdalen was of the House of
Benjamin. Royal blood.

TEABING (over)

Remember, Jesus was descended from
King David himself.

TEABING

Literally King of the Jews.

Teabing smiles at her. He hits a switch at the base of
the monitor, now writes on the touch-screen with
his finger.

TEABING

My dear, the word in French for the
Holy Grail?

SOPHIE

Saint-Graal.

TEABING

From the Middle English *Sangreal.*

He has written that word on his impromptu chalk board.

TEABING

Now as two words. Can you translate
for our friend?

He draws a line with his finger, separating *Sang* and *Real*.

SOPHIE

Sang. Real. It means. Royal blood.

TEABING

When the legend speaks of the chalice that held the blood of Christ, it speaks, in fact, of the female womb that carried Jesus' royal bloodline.

SOPHIE

But how could Christ have a bloodline unless — ?

LANGDON

Now come on, Leigh.

SOPHIE

Unless Christ had a child.

TEABING

Mary was pregnant at the time of the crucifixion.

See Mary in plain robes on a road as soldiers pass in the other direction, Jerusalem gone small now in the distance.

TEABING *(over)*

For her own safety and that of Christ's unborn child, Mary fled the Holy Land and came to France. Here she is said to have given birth to a daughter.

A midwife moves into a small bedroom, holding a bowl of steaming water as Mary's pregnant belly heaves in the foreground.

TEABING *(over)*

Sarah.

This tiny girl lies peaceful on her mother's stomach.

SOPHIE

They know the child's name?

LANGDON

A girl child. That would have been adding insult to injury.

SOPHIE

Why?

LANGDON

In paganism, transcendence was achieved by joining male to female.

SOPHIE

People found God through sex?

LANGDON

Yes. And women were worshiped as a route to heaven. But the new church had a monopoly on salvation through Jesus.

TEABING
He who holds the keys to heaven rules
the world.

LANGDON
To the Church this made women quite
a threat.

*Inquisitors carry a woman from her home past her
WAILING children and husband.*

LANGDON
The Catholic Inquisition would soon
publish what may be the most blood-
soaked book in human history —

Women are carried naked in cages, on soldiers' shoulders.

TEABING
Malleus Maleficarum, instructing the
clergy on how to locate, torture, and
kill all free-thinking women —

*Women are stoned to death; fall past us, drowned,
through deep, clear water.*

EXT. CHATEAU VILLETTE – NIGHT
Silas watches through the window.

LANGDON
In three centuries of witch hunts they
burned over fifty thousand women at the
stake.

TEABING
At least. Some say millions.

INT. CHATEAU VILLETTE – BALLROOM – NIGHT
Sophie stares at them, stunned.

LANGDON
Imagine, then, that an heir to Christ's
throne might live on in a female child.

TEABING
You asked what would be worth killing for? Witness the greatest cover-up in
human history. Not only was Jesus Christ
married, he was a father. Mary Magdalen
was the Holy Vessel, the Chalice. This is the
secret the Priory of Sion has defended for
over twenty centuries. They are the guardians of the bloodline, the keepers of the
proof of our true past. They are the pro-
tectors of the living descendants of Jesus
Christ and Mary Magdalen.

The moment lasts, so silent you can almost hear history.

SOPHIE
She must have been terribly alone.

Both men look startled.

TEABING
She lived out her days in hiding. So,
yes. I suppose she must have.

*The top of a beautifully painted sarcophagus is
lowered over a resting body, her face shrouded, her
tomb in shadows.* (OVER) A sudden BUZZ from
the INTERCOM.

TEABING
Sometimes I wonder who is serving
whom?

(OVER) A longer, more alarming BUZZ.

TEABING
His sauces are not *that* fantastic.

Teabing steps to the intercom panel.

INT. CHATEAU VILLETTE – KITCHEN
Remy stands at the intercom. In the background, two
faces on the TV screen behind a NEWSCASTER:
Sophie and Langdon.

REMY
Yes. They are on the news programs
now. Two channels.

A shape moves past behind him, white and fast, deeper
into the house. Like a ghost. Remy spins but the room is
empty.

INT. CHATEAU VILLETTE – BALLROOM – NIGHT
Teabing turns from the wall.

TEABING
You have not been honest with me.

His face is red, practically spitting.

TEABING
Your pictures are on the television.
You're wanted for four murders.

SOPHIE
Four?

LANGDON
. . . That's why Vernet said killing
spree —

TEABING
You come into my home, playing on
my passions for the Grail —

LANGDON
It's why he needed you, Sophie —

TEABING
You will leave my house —

LANGDON
The others were already dead —

TEABING

I'm calling the police —

LANGDON

Sauniere needed you to take over for
him —

TEABING

Immediately —

LANGDON

Leigh, listen —

TEABING

You have nothing to say that I —

LANGDON

Jacques Sauniere was her grandfather.

Sudden, real force.

LANGDON

You're the obsessive Priory scholar.
Do you still keep lists of who could be
in the Priory?

Teabing stares at him.

LANGDON

Jacques Sauniere was on one of your
lists, wasn't he?

Robert is looking at Sophie, pieces falling into place.

LANGDON

He was on your list of who could be
Grand Master.

SOPHIE

What?

LANGDON

I bet he was right at the top.

He's certainly got Teabing's attention.

LANGDON

Consider. *Four* men murdered. The
number of the guardians.

MYSTERIOUS POV – Watching Langdon from the
shadows.

LANGDON

What if the Priory was compromised?
The other *sénéchaux* already dead?

BACK TO SCENE.

LANGDON

What if you were dying yourself?
You'd have to pass the secret on to
someone you could trust. Someone
outside the society. Maybe someone
whose training you had begun but
never finished.

TEABING

This ruse is pathetic.

LANGDON

Not really.

From his pocket, Langdon withdraws a familiar wooden
box.

TEABING

No. Impossible.

Leigh can barely pull his eyes off the box.

TEABING
Can you really . . . ? Is that the keystone?

LANGDON
I'll even show it to you, Leigh. If you'll
just tell us what the hell it's for.

EXT. CHATEAU VILLETTE – ACCESS ROAD – NIGHT
Three police cruisers come to a stop on the country
road, bubble lights dark. Collet and several officers
emerge.

COLLET
Orders are we wait.

One cop moves in close to Collet.

COP
**It doesn't make sense. What's he think-
ing? The truck is here. They're inside.
We can take them.**

COLLET
Fache says we wait. So I wait.

But Collet is clearly frustrated himself.

INT. CHATEAU VILLETTE – LIBRARY – NIGHT
Dark wood. Rustic eagle-claw rocker. Fire in a giant
hearth. Sophie watches Teabing, in white gloves, gingerly
examine the box on a light table with long tweezers.

TEABING
As legend promised. It hides beneath
the rose.

He touches the rose inlay gently, in full revery.

LANGDON
Like this.

Langdon flips it open with his hand. Leigh glares at him.

LANGDON
Leigh. Please.

TEABING
Yes. Of course. The keystone is a map.
A map to find the Holy Grail.

Teabing shifts his focus to Sophie.

TEABING
To be trained by the Grand Master
himself. Did he pass down the fleur-de-
lis? Is that how you found this?

Teabing's hands are on the box, his eyes still on her.

TEABING
He must have sung you the riddle
songs. I've learned some.

Teabing HUMS. *Sauniere appears in the corner of the room,
standing over a young Sophie, HUMMING the same tune.*

TEABING
Can you keep secrets? Can you know
a thing and never say it again?

*Another Sauniere, finger to his lips, and another young
Sophie.*

TEABING
And codes. I imagine they lay down
for you like lovers.

*A third Sauniere and young Sophie work a puzzle
all of white.*

TEABING
A *sénéchal*. A guardian of the Grail.
Right here in my home.

The blood has run out of her face. She looks to
Langdon.

SOPHIE
Tell him. Please. I don't know any of this.

But even Sophie sounds less than entirely sure.

LANGDON
Leigh, it's not that simple —

A shape SMASHES into Langdon, hands going hard
around his throat, SMASHING him into the wall.
Langdon slumps.

SILAS
God alone judges the worthy.

Teabing sets the box on the table.

TEABING
Faith has no earthly price.

Silas's eyes narrow at the familiar verse.

SILAS
And no bounty save its own reward.

Teabing slides his cane into Silas's leg. Silas SCREAMS as Teabing now hits his crotch, his neck. Silas falls, his gun FIRING as he hits the ground, window EXPLODING.

Teabing has fallen too. But before Silas can look up, Sophie grabs his head and SLAMS it to the floor, once, twice, KNOCKING him out cold.

TEABING
Well well, my dear.

SOPHIE
Robert!

SILAS
Do not move, woman.

Silas stands pointing the gun at Sophie.

SILAS
Cripple. Put the box on the table.

TEABING
This trifle? Perhaps we could make a financial arrangement.

SILAS
(lethal)
Put it on the table.

Teabing notes a trickle of blood running down Silas's leg.

TEABING
You will not succeed. Only the worthy can unlock the stone.

EXT. CHATEAU VILLETTE – MAIN GATE – SAME TIME
Collet stands outside his car, on his radio. (OVER) A
GUNSHOT.

COLLET
Tie on the gate. Pull it down.

INT. CHATEAU VILLETTE – LIBRARY – NIGHT
Remy runs into the doorway, stops cold, stands
speechless.

TEABING
Make yourself useful, fool, get something to restrain this monster.

Sophie is with Langdon at the wall. He is trying to
get up. He touches the back of his head to find
blood there.

LANGDON
Okay . . . ?

In front of him lies an unconscious albino, chin split
open, robe over his right thigh soaked with blood.

LANGDON
Wow. Saved by Leigh Teabing.

TEABING
The benefit of my condition. Everyone
underestimates me.

Remy has returned. All now begin binding the monk's
wrists, ankles, mouth with duct tape.

SOPHIE
Higher. Above the joint.

Remy already knew. The rest oblige.

TEABING
Fortunately, a dragon most easy to slay.
He was wearing a cilice.

SOPHIE
A what?

Teabing pulls aside the monk's robes to show sharp steel.

LANGDON
Inflicts pain so the wearer will suf-
fer as Jesus suffered. Not so common
these days.

TEABING
Opus Dei.

LANGDON
Fache is Opus Dei.
(to Teabing)
The cop who's been chasing us. He was
wearing the Cross in the World.

TEABING
The reach of the devout is long.

LANGDON
And without mercy.

Makeup

Many tests were done to come up with the right look for the Silas character. Makeup artist Veronica Brebner spent two and a half hours a day on the process, starting with the application of various blue-tinted foundations to balance Paul Bettany's red complexion and minimize his freckles. Then blemishes were re-created, such as dark circles under his eyes. Lastly, his wig was applied—dying Paul's own hair was ruled out early in the process, as it could never get quite white enough without burning his scalp.

A shared understanding of this old verse.

SOPHIE
Robert.

Sophie points to the desk. On a security monitor the gate, attached by chains to straining police cars, is coming down.

TEABING
I must say. You two are anything but dull.

LANGDON
Leigh. You want what's in this box.
And we need help getting out of here.

On the monitor, the cars come spilling through the gate.

TEABING
Well, actually, I do . . .

That humor, back in his eyes.

TEABING
. . . have a plane.

INT. CHATEAU VILLETTE – FOYER/STAIRS/HALLWAY – NIGHT
The door FLIES open. Collet and his men burst in, guns drawn. Empty. Dead silence. Then (OVER) VOICES upstairs, hurried, the unmistakable SOUNDS of people on the move. Collet gives orders by signaling with his hands.

FAVOR Collet as he and his MEN mount the stairs, head fast down the long hallway towards the VOICES growing louder.

Two men flank the last door, VOICES LOUD on the other side, as Collet KICKS open the door, gun drawn to find . . .

INT. CHATEAU VILLETTE – GUEST BEDROOM – NIGHT
No sign of life. The VOICES come from a speaker set into the wall. Collet crosses to the intercom panel. *Study. Kitchen. Laundry.* There, a red light shines beside *Barn.*

COLLET
Merde!

An ENGINE GUNS. Collet moves to the window.

Below, a Range Rover is flying out of the barn towards the forest beyond.

EXT. CHATEAU VILLETTE – FOREST – NIGHT
The black SUV, headlights off, is tearing across a moonlit clearing towards a jagged silhouette of woods ahead.

INT. – RANGE ROVER – MOVING – NIGHT
Remy drives, Langdon beside him. Teabing and Sophie in back. The car BLOWS into the moonlit forest.

          LANGDON
Jesus.

          TEABING
Apropos.

Langdon can't help but flinch as branches SCRAPE the front windshield and WHIP against the sides of the vehicle.

          LANGDON
Easy!

(OVER) A GROWL of rage as Silas tries to free himself. Teabing turns to the gagged, bound monk through the dog screen. Teabing's TONE is startlingly lethal.

          TEABING
    I can't imagine your complaint. I
    would be within my rights . . .

Teabing raises the pistol.

          TEABING
    . . . to shoot you and let you rot in my woods.

But the monk has, in fact, fallen silent. Teabing slips his gun back into his jacket pocket.

          TEABING
Better.

          LANGDON
Man.

A darkness in Sophie's eyes as she focuses on Silas.

          SOPHIE
Opus Dei? What is it?

          LANGDON
Opus Dei is a prelature to the Vatican.

          SOPHIE
You're saying the Vatican is killing people? For this box?

          TEABING
No. Not the Vatican. Not Opus Dei.

Teabing takes a beat.

          TEABING
We are in the middle of a war. One that has gone on forever. On one side stands the Priory. On the other is an ancient group of despots with members hidden in high-ranking positions throughout the Church. This Council of Shadows tries to destroy the Grail documents as devoutly as the Priory fights to protect them.

Teabing looks out the back window.

          TEABING
Some say their mission is darker still. That the hunt for the Magdalen has never ended and that throughout

history they seek out and kill the living
descendants of Jesus Christ.

SOPHIE
That's insane.

TEABING
Is it? How many atrocities and scan-
dals has the Catholic Church ratio-
nalized in its time? What happens if
persuasive, scientific evidence emerges
showing the Church's version of
Christ's story as inaccurate? What if
the world discovers that the greatest
story ever told is a lie?

LANGDON
The Vatican faces a crisis of faith
unprecedented in two thousand years.

REMY
I've got a signal now, sir, it's ringing.

Remy hands the phone to Teabing.

TEABING
Richard, so sorry. I have grown tired
of the weather in France. Please ready
the plane for . . .

Teabing looks at Langdon, who shrugs.

TEABING
Zurich. We love Zurich.

EXT. CHATEAU VILLETTE – NIGHT
Collet is directing his men to make a grounds
search. Fache's car pulls in, the captain
emerging. Furious.

FACHE
**What the hell do you mean you lost
them? Collet, you —**

COLLET
You **lost them. You don't let anybody
breathe. You control every step of this
investigation. You're acting like you've lost
your mind. What is it with these two birds?**

Fache frowns. For a moment Collet sees the man he knew.

COLLET
Bezu —

A COP appears.

COP
**Interpol just registered a new flight
plan from Le Bourget.**

Fache's eyes are instantly dark with purpose again.

FACHE
**Did they take the old man who lives
here? Is he in on it? Find out!**

Fache is already heading to his car. Collet stares after.

EXT. HAWKER 731 – BOURGET AIRFIELD RUNWAY – NIGHT – TAXIING
The plane makes a slow turn onto the runway.

INT. HAWKER 731 – RUNWAY – NIGHT – MOVING
Teabing and Remy sit in the front square. Langdon sits in the rear with Sophie, her gaze still fixed on Silas.

She unbuckles her seat belt and moves quickly to the rear alcove, stares down at the monk, her eyes burning.

> **CAPTAIN** (*over*)
> All passengers must be seated for takeoff.

Sophie RIPS the duct tape off the monk's mouth roughly. Silas can't stifle a GROAN of pain. He looks up at her.

> **SOPHIE**
> Did you kill Jacques Sauniere?

> **CAPTAIN** (*over*)
> Will the lady please be seated.

> **SOPHIE**
> Did you kill Jacques Sauniere?

> **SILAS**
> I am the messenger of God.

She SLAPS him hard, in the face.

> **SOPHIE**
> Did you kill my grandfather?

> **SILAS**
> I am the messenger.

She SLAPS him again.

Imagine Entertainment executive Anna Culp and Dan Brown on the set of Teabing's Hawker aircraft.

> **SILAS**
> Each breath you take is sin. No shadow will be safe again. You will be hunted by angels.

Enough to freeze your blood or mine. Not Sophie's.

> **SOPHIE**
> You believe in God? He knows you. Your God doesn't forgive murderers. Your God burns them.

Her force is unimaginable. Two old powers met and matched.

> **CAPTAIN** (*over*)
> Miss, if you don't sit down I'll have to abort the takeoff.

> **LANGDON**
> Sophie.

She slaps the tape back over Silas's mouth, stumbles to her seat just as, out the windows, the ground falls away.

INT. CASTLE GANDOLFO – BILLIARD ROOM – NIGHT
That young member of the council ENTERS, a briefcase in his hands. He simply sets it down, bows slightly, and backs out.

> PREFECT
> What will you do?

> ARINGAROSA
> Destroy the documents and the sarcophagus, of course.

> PREFECT
> And the heir? Will you exercise the final edict? Spill his blood?

Aringarosa returns to his game, takes another shot.

> ARINGAROSA
> There would be no need. With the sarcophagus destroyed, DNA testing would be impossible. There will be no way to prove a living bloodline.

The Prefect simply fixes him with his stare.

> ARINGAROSA
> Salvatore, what harm can he do? He doesn't even know his own identity.

> PREFECT
> But if he discovered who he is?

> ARINGAROSA
> Once the proof is gone, it would be his word against the Church.

> PREFECT
> But if you had to? Would you do as councils have done before us?

> ARINGAROSA
> Christ sacrificed his life for the betterment of humanity.

Aringarosa nods, melancholy.

> ARINGAROSA
> Why shouldn't his seed?

EXT. HAWKER 731 – NIGHT – FLYING
The plane is climbing towards the hanging sea of clouds.

INT. HAWKER 731 – FLYING

Teabing is using hanging leather ceiling straps to walk himself to the bathroom. Sophie is staring out the window.

TEABING
Try *Paris*. And if that doesn't work, try it in reverse.

Langdon works the cryptex as Teabing vanishes into the loo.

SOPHIE
Robert, when we land, you must go straight to your embassy.

LANGDON
Is that so?

Despite her bravado, Silas has had an effect on her.

SOPHIE
Don't you see it? They never wanted you. Maybe even Fache did not. It's all about this idiotic little box.

LANGDON
That's not too flattering.

SOPHIE
Crazy old man.

No contempt this time, just sadness.

SOPHIE
Why leave me with this? I should just throw it away.

LANGDON
He trusted you.

She opens her mouth to respond. Closes it instead.

SOPHIE
A guardian of the Holy Grail. It sounds so stupid.

LANGDON
Quite an honor, if you take it seriously.

SOPHIE
He took it seriously enough to get himself killed, no?

She looks at Langdon.

LANGDON
Not him, Sophie. You.

She stares at him.

SOPHIE
He was the only family I knew. But maybe I didn't know him at all.

She takes a moment.

SOPHIE
I am his marionette. Like a girl again, just with no gift at the end.
(*a beat*)
But you've done enough, Robert.

LANGDON
I'm still not sure why Sauniere picked me to help you, Sophie. But I'm not going to leave you alone in this.

SOPHIE
Two marionettes, then.

She smiles.

                    SOPHIE
        Maybe this is why he chose you, no?
        Because you will stay.

INT. BOURGET AIRFIELD – CONTROL TOWER – NIGHT
The first hints of dawn spread through the 360-degree windows. Fache and a lone, cigarette-smoking CONTROLLER are in mid-conversation.

                    CONTROLLER
        Ten minutes.

He shrugs. As if describing the weather. Fache smiles.

                    FACHE
        Reconsider.

                    CONTROLLER
        I'm on break. Come back in ten minutes.

Fache shrugs, starts to turn, returning with linked hands, savage, SMASHING the controller in the face. The man goes down on his knees, blood spilling through his fingers.

                    CONTROLLER
        **My nose, my nose. What's wrong with
        you, you bastard? Oh God, my nose.**

Fache towers over him.

                    FACHE
        The flight plan, please.

Fache begins to savagely kick the felled controller.

                    FACHE
        The. Flight. Plan. Please.

INT. HAWKER 731 – FLYING – NIGHT
The wooden box sits on a folded-out table between Sophie, Teabing, and Langdon. Remy checks Silas's bonds in the background.

                    LANGDON
        How many more are there?

Sophie glances at a pad beside them. Covered with five-letter words, all scratched out.

                    SOPHIE
        Including backwards?

Langdon shoots her a look. She smiles.

                    TEABING
              (working the cryptex)
        Not *Horus. Stone.*

Sophie crosses out *Horus* on the pad. Writes *Voute*.

                    SOPHIE
        What happened to her?

Both look at Sophie.

                    SOPHIE
        Mary.

                    TEABING
        No one knows. For years men and women
        journeyed to worship at the tomb of the
        outcast one. To kneel beside the bones
        of Mary Magdalen was to remember all
        those who have been robbed of power and
        oppressed, to pay tribute to those countless
        souls discarded by history. But the zealous
        hounded her still, even in death, and her
        sarcophagus was finally lost to time.

The Da Vinci Rainbow

As filming proceeds, revisions of the script are reflected in ever-changing colors, each representing the date of the new pages. *The Da Vinci Code* had twenty-five revisions over six months. It began with an all white script, but by the end of shooting, the story pages appeared as a virtual rainbow.

SOPHIE
What's really hidden here? Proof of a
life lived in whispers?

LANGDON
Whispers?

Langdon picks up the box and opens the lid. He shifts its
position until light catches a small hole on the underside.

LANGDON
I need something small. No. Wait.

He lifts his pencil, inspects the sharp graphite.

TEABING
What are you doing?

LANGDON
At the house you said, "hides beneath
the rose."

Robert inserts the pencil point into the tiny hole.

TEABING
No, no. Careful.

LANGDON
Whispers. In Latin, *sub rosa*. Literal translation . . .

He pushes. A small section of wood, like a puzzle piece,
falls onto his lap. He lifts the wooden shape of a rose.

TEABING
Under the rose.

There, engraved in the wood, written in immaculate hand,
four lines of text in an alien language. Langdon smiles.

LANGDON
We need a mirror.

INT. HAWKER 731 – KITCHEN ALCOVE – MOMENTS LATER
In London lies a knight a pope interred.
His labor's fruit a Holy wrath incurred.
You seek the orb that ought be on his tomb.
It speaks of Rosy flesh and seeded womb.

TEABING (over)
In the style of Leonardo himself.

PULL BACK TO REVEAL all three standing,
holding the puzzle piece up to the mirror.
Teabing hangs on to one of his straps.

TEABING
He was quite marvelous, wasn't he?
Your grandfather.

Langdon watches Sophie take a beat before answering.

SOPHIE
I suppose he was.

TEABING
In London lies a knight a pope interred.

LANGDON
A knight whose funeral was presided
over by a pope?

TEABING
Always the optimist.

Langdon's smile is humorless.

LANGDON
A knight *killed* by a pope, then.

SOPHIE
But there must be hundreds?

TEABING
The Priory knights weren't just any knights.

LANGDON
Templars.

Teabing is nodding.

TEABING
And there's just one place to bury a Templar knight in London.

LANGDON
Temple Church.

TEABING
Temple Church.

Teabing begins hoisting himself towards the cockpit door.

TEABING
Richard and I are about to discuss a new flight plan.

LANGDON
Leigh. Harboring and transporting fugitives. You're already implicated enough.

Teabing turns back to Langdon, hanging from his straps.

TEABING
You and I, Robert, we have observed history. Time has been our looking glass. What a luxury I thought that was, to grow smug with perspective. But you get older . . . Observation is an indulgence, old friend. And a callow one at that. We are in history now. Making it. Living it. *Implicated?* I am on a Grail quest. Forgive me, Robert. But you two may well have given this old man the greatest night of his life. Thank you.

He's already turned towards the cockpit.

TEABING
He's going to want more money.

Langdon can't help but smile at his old friend as he goes.

EXT. HAWKER 731 – FLYING
The first rays of daylight break on the plane as it banks.

INT. LE BOURGET AIRFIELD – HANGAR – DAWN
Fache stands by the detritus from Teabing's abandoned Range Rover, everything spilled out in a reckless search.

COLLET *(over)*
This must be that new procedure for preserving chain of evidence.

Fache turns to find Collet in the door, walking smoke cloud, puffing away. Fache's eyes are ringed, exhausted.

FACHE
I've lost them. They flew to Switzerland. No extradition.

Collet nods. Something else in Fache's eyes. Desperation.

this man's heart. That he would keep
killing. He said I had to stop him. He
charged me to stop him. Now who
have I failed, Jerome? The bishop?
God himself?

Fache holds his face in praying hands. Collet stares
at him.

> COLLET
> They changed their flight plan. They're
> going to London.

Fache just stares.

> COLLET
> Go on. I'll take care of the controller.
> Maybe he needs a few extra euros.
> You're paying. Just tell me next time.

Fache has turned, already on his phone, expression hard.

> FACHE
> I'll be in London in less than an hour.

INT. POLICE CAR – BIGGIN HILL – DRIVING
A young CAPTAIN leads several squad cars. In
the distance a familiar Hawker glides towards the
airport ahead.

> CAPTAIN
> I have them. Tower, relay Hawker to
> land and hold on tarmac.

INT. HAWKER 731 – DESCENDING – DAY
Sophie turns back from the window, exchanging a look
of concern with Langdon.

Teabing finishes speaking quietly to Remy; the manser-
vant crosses towards Silas, pulling out a glinting knife.

> COLLET
> The controller filed charges. Ari was
> on dispatch. He called me.

Collet stares at his old friend.

> COLLET
> Bezu, what's going on?

Fache takes a beat before responding.

> FACHE
> You know that I am Opus Dei?

Collet's shrug says *Of course.*

> FACHE
> Last night, an important man calls me.
> The bishop of my order. He says I will
> soon learn of a murder. Four murders.
> He says the killer came to him in con-
> fession. His name is Robert Langdon.
> The bishop broke his vows to tell me.
> He said I could not imagine the evil in

B. HAWKER JET LOWERS INTO SHOT.

A. OVER SHOULDER SOPHIE — SEES A PROCESSION OF POLICE CARS, DOME LIGHTS FLASHING.

EXT. BIGGIN HILL – DAY
The Hawker touches down, police cars closing. Instead of breaking, the jet accelerates towards a hangar.

INT. HAWKER 731 – BIGGIN HILL AIRPORT – TARMAC – DAY
Sophie stares out the window. The string of police car lights spin to life, SIRENS wailing as they give chase.

EXT. BIGGIN HILL AIRPORT – TARMAC – SECONDS LATER
The police sedans race after the taxiing plane. The Hawker is still five hundred yards ahead as it vanishes into the hangar.

INT. BIGGIN HILL AIRPORT – HANGAR – SECONDS LATER
Cars SCREECH to a stop, spilling cops as the Hawker completes its 180-degree rotation and POWERS DOWN.

Storyboards by Robert Ballantyne.

147

The police position themselves around the plane as the hatch POPS and Teabing begins down the distending gangway.

> **TEABING**
> Good morning. Did that old cannabis charge finally catch up with me?

Remy appears behind Teabing, descending.

> **POLICE CAPTAIN**
> I'm to take you and the other two on board into custody.

> **TEABING**
> Sadly, I have a medical appointment I cannot afford to miss.

> **REMY**
> I'll fetch the car, sir.

Remy hits the tarmac. Starts towards a parked Daimler.

> **POLICE CAPTAIN**
> This is serious, sir. The French police are on their way.

> **TEABING**
> There is no one else on board. Please, look for yourselves.

Cops start towards the plane.

INT. DAIMLER – CONTINUOUS
Teabing climbs into the passenger seat beside Remy. Three cops block the car.

> **REMY**
> I could run them over.

Teabing shoots him a look. The moment lasts. Then the captain emerges from the plane. Shakes his head.

> **POLICE CAPTAIN**
> A bad tip. Let them go.

> **TEABING**
> (calling out)
> The French cannot be trusted!

As the car pulls onto the tarmac, Leigh lowers the divider.

> **TEABING** (over)
> Everyone comfy? Need biscuits?

On the floor of the passenger compartment sit Sophie, Langdon, and the bound and gagged monk.

> **LANGDON**
> They didn't notice the skid marks.

Teabing glances out the back window.

Plane and cops vanish. A ghost plane taxis into the hangar, hatch popping as the plane stops halfway through its turn.

Ghosts Langdon and Sophie drag ghost Silas down the gangway and behind the car as the jet engines ROAR to life again, plane resuming its turn just as the ghost cops race in.

> **TEABING**
> People rarely see what is right before their eyes, don't you find?

The hangar recedes into the distance.

INT. CASTLE GANDOLFO – STONE STEPS – MORNING
The Prefect comes downstairs in his night-shirt to find Aringarosa carrying the briefcase out to the car.

> **ARINGAROSA**
> I fly to London. The Teacher is waiting for me there.

Aringarosa swells with pride.

> **ARINGAROSA**
> He has chosen a house of Opus Dei to make the exchange. Mere currency for the location of the Grail. Imagine it.

The Prefect follows Aringarosa out the open door . . .

EXT. CASTLE GANDOLFO – MORNING – CONTINUOUS
The Prefect faces Aringarosa in first light.

> **PREFECT**
> In my world, you would be Pope for this, Manuel.

ARINGAROSA
God's will be done.

The Prefect makes the sign of a cross on his forehead.

PREFECT
Of course, should anything go —

ARINGAROSA
Yes. This council does not exist. As we never have.

PREFECT
Heaven protect you, old friend.

EXT. LONDON – MORNING – HELICOPTER – ESTABLISHING
Swoop down through mighty bridges and snaking blue water of the Thames into the bustling city's streets.

EXT. SIDE STREET – MORNING
The Daimler pulls to a stop on the waking street. Sophie, Teabing, and Langdon emerge. Teabing turns to Remy.

TEABING
Best to avoid the police.

Remy watches them go.

EXT. TEMPLE CHURCH – GROUNDS – MORNING – WALKING
They cross a small garden and climb narrow stairs.

TEABING
(off the narrow walls)
I must say, Robert, I'm quite impressed with the way you withstood my little plane.

Teabing notes Sophie's puzzled expression.

TEABING
Did he never tell you? When he was a boy, young Robert fell into a well. How old were you?

LANGDON
Seven.

TEABING
Treading water all night, screaming his lungs out into the echoes screaming back. When they found him he was nearly catatonic.

SOPHIE
Oh.

The narrow sides of the stairs are suddenly close well-walls, WORDS ECHOING, now, against the sweating stone.

LANGDON
It was a long time ago.

TEABING
Tsk-tsk, Robert, you of all people shouldn't be one to dismiss the influence of the past.

They emerge into a courtyard.

EXT. TEMPLE CHURCH – MORNING
Circular. Rough hewn. More military stronghold than place of worship. They approach the stone edifice.

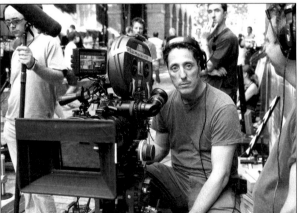

Temple Church

Temple Church was what is known as a practical location—meaning that all shots from the Temple Church scenes were actually filmed there. To light the church, director of photography Sal Totino (left) used large, dramatic streaks of light to paint the frame. The only alteration was minor set dressing—for example, two light-rubber effigies were brought in and used during the scene so that Audrey Tautou could fall on them without actually hurting herself.

LANGDON
I always forget it's right here.

TEABING
Built in 1185. Modern London sprang up right around it.

SOPHIE
Sir Leigh, why has the Priory kept the Grail documents secret all these years?

TEABING
I don't know. Many of us believed the Priory's sacred charge was to reveal the heir at the dawn of the new millen-nium. Now some say they have reverted to an older edict, that the Priory waits for the heir to reveal himself. Especially odd considering legend suggests the heir may not be aware of his own true identity.

Langdon is inspecting a bulletin board on the wall.

LANGDON
Says they don't open for an hour.

Sophie pushes old wood and the door swings, CREAKING open.

INT. TEMPLE CHURCH – DAY
The sanctuary is small. Bleak, despite the already lit candles. Langdon, Teabing, and Sophie ENTER.

> **TEABING**
> Hello?

No answer. Sophie glances around, shadows everywhere.

> **SOPHIE**
> Why do they make them so scary?

> **TEABING**
> Anybody home?

Again nothing. They move deeper into this ancient space.

> **SOPHIE**
> It's cold.

On the floor ahead lie ten stone knights. Life-sized figures, deeply weathered, and yet each unique.

> **LANGDON**
> In London lies a knight a pope interred.

> **TEABING**
> Yes.

> **LANGDON**
> So which tomb has an orb?

INT. TEMPLE CHURCH – MORNING
Langdon and Teabing stand amid the old stone knights. Sophie circles the perimeter, uncomfortable.

> **LANGDON**
> Three have their legs extended while two have them crossed. Means they've been to Jerusalem.

INT. DAIMLER – FLEET STREET – DAY
Remy sits in the driver's seat. He stares into the mirror. Silas now sits up in the backseat, still bound, staring back.

Remy reaches to the glove compartment. He flips it open. Inside we see two guns, Teabing's and Remy's, as well as a familiar knife.

TEABING
Two wear tunics over armor while two
wear ankle length robes.

As Sophie walks the curvature of the chamber, sinister
carvings stare down at her.

LANGDON
Two clutch swords.

TEABING
Two pray.

Gargoyles and demons grin at her.

LANGDON
One has his arms at his sides.

TEABING
And that fellow's vanished entirely.

Monsters taunt with crooked stone mouths.

LANGDON
But I see no orbs that ought be on a
tomb. *Ought* be on a tomb. Are we
looking for a missing orb?

TEABING
There must be something over here.

LANGDON
(beat)
They're not tombs.

He has lifted an information brochure.

TEABING
Of course they are.

LANGDON
(off a wall plaque)
Effigies. No bodies underneath.

SOPHIE
This place is wrong.

Clouds cover the sun outside, darkening the room to night.

SOPHIE
Can we go now? We should go.

Suddenly, movement. Silas explodes out of the darkness, already dragging Sophie backwards into the shadows, a glinting knife to her throat.

SILAS
Where is the keystone? Do not test me.

He presses the knife harder into her throat, tiny beads of blood forming where skin meets steel. SHOUTS overlap.

SILAS
I will kill her —

LANGDON
Let her go —

TEABING

Don't hurt her —

SILAS

Where is the keystone —

TEABING

Stop this —

SILAS

Give me the keystone —

LANGDON

It's right here.

Langdon holds out the cryptex.

LANGDON

Let the others go. You and I can settle
this ourselves.

(OVER) A CLICK. WIDER.

TEABING

Remy?

Remy has ENTERED the church behind Langdon, gun
in his hand.

LANGDON

Remy, don't. They're too close together.
You don't have a clear shot.

REMY

No.

The gun comes up, pointing directly at Langdon's head.

REMY

I do.

TEABING

Stop that. What are you doing?

Remy reaches down, takes the box from Langdon's hand.

REMY

Thank you, Professor. For a moment
this was getting complicated.

Silas shoves Sophie towards the men. Remy corrals the
captives with his gun.

TEABING

This is absurd. What in God's name —

Remy BACKHANDS him across the mouth.

REMY

That was satisfying. I'm glad this
bullshit is over.

Sophie stands beside Langdon.

> **REMY**
> One Grail historian is quite enough.

Remy points the gun at Langdon.

> **REMY**
> Throw Teabing in the trunk.

Silas shoves Sophie to the ground. Langdon rushes to her.

> **TEABING**
> What? No!

Silas begins dragging Teabing towards the side door.

Remy locks eyes with Langdon. He CLICKS back the hammer.

> **REMY**
> Sorry.

(OVER) A sudden EXPLOSION of WINGS as two doves fly from an upper balcony, their BEATING WINGS echoing through the space.

Sophie pulls Langdon's hand, racing fast past pews. They whip out the door, bullets EXPLODING ancient stone behind them.

EXT. TEMPLE LANE – DAY – CONTINUOUS
Remy whips out into the narrow alley, gun drawn,

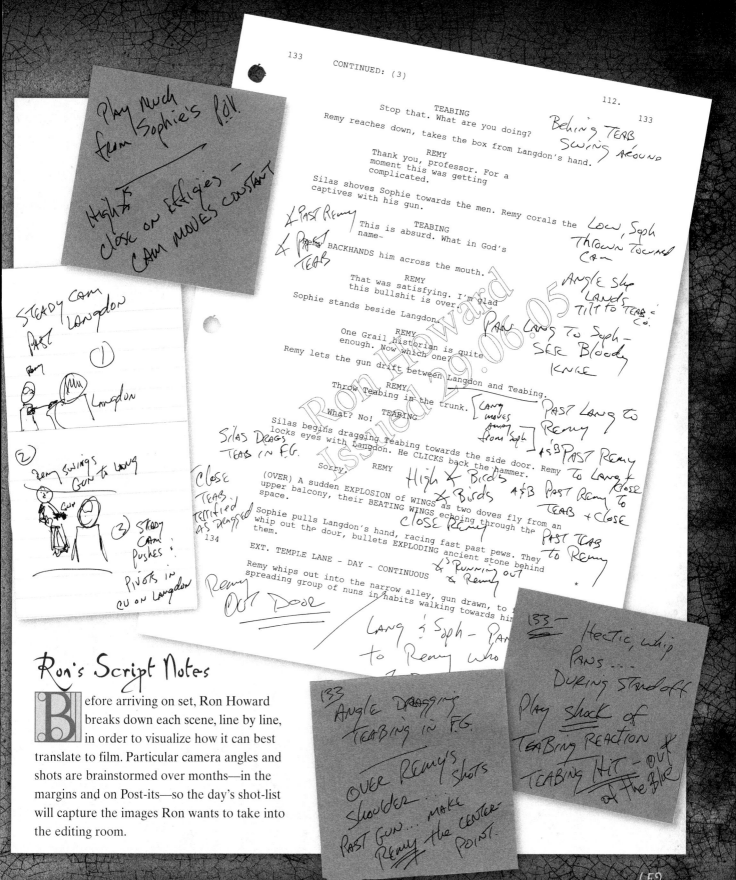

133
CONTINUED: (3)

112.
133

TEABING
Stop that. What are you doing?

Remy reaches down, takes the box from Langdon's hand.

REMY
Thank you, professor. For a
moment this was getting
complicated

Silas shoves Sophie towards the men. Remy corals the
captives with his gun.

TEABING
This is absurd. What in God's
name—

Remy BACKHANDS him across the mouth.

REMY
That was satisfying. I'm glad
this bullshit is over.

Sophie stands beside Langdon.

REMY
One Grail historian is quite
enough. Now which one?

Remy lets the gun drift between Langdon and Teabing.

REMY
Throw Teabing in the trunk.

TEABING
What? No!

Silas begins dragging Teabing towards the side door. Remy
locks eyes with Langdon. He CLICKS back the hammer.

REMY
Sorry.

(OVER) A sudden EXPLOSION of WINGS as two doves fly from an
upper balcony, their BEATING WINGS echoing through the
space.

Sophie pulls Langdon's hand, racing fast past pews. They
whip out the door, bullets EXPLODING ancient stone behind
them.

134
EXT. TEMPLE LANE - DAY - CONTINUOUS

Remy whips out into the narrow alley, gun drawn, to
spreading group of nuns in habits walking towards him

Handwritten annotations:

- Behind TEAB SWING AROUND
- Low, Soph Thrown Toward Cam
- Angle she Lands TILT to TEAB & Co.
- PANS Lang To Soph — SEE Bloody KNEE
- X PAST Remy
- X Remy PAST TEAB
- PAST Lang to Remy
- 1's PAST Remy To Lang & CLOSE
- High & Birds A&B PAST Remy to TEAB + CLOSE
- High & Birds X Birds CLOSE Remy
- PAST TEAB to Remy
- [Lang moves away from Soph]
- Silas DRAGS TEAB IN F.G.
- CLOSE TEAB: TERRIFIED AS DRAGGED
- 1's RUNNING OUT & Remy
- Remy OUT DOOR
- Lang & Soph — PAN to Remy who

Ron Howard *Issued 2009.06.05* (watermark)

Ron's Script Notes

Before arriving on set, Ron Howard breaks down each scene, line by line, in order to visualize how it can best translate to film. Particular camera angles and shots are brainstormed over months—in the margins and on Post-its—so the day's shot-list will capture the images Ron wants to take into the editing room.

Post-it note (top left):
Play much from Sophie's P.O.V.
High's
Close on effigies — CAM MOVES CONSTANT

Note card (left):
STEADY CAM PAST Langdon
① Remy → Langdon
② Remy SWINGS Gun to Lang
③ STEADY CAM pushes & PIVOTS in CU on Langdon

Post-it (bottom center):
133
ANGLE DRAGGING TEABING in F.G.
OVER Remy's Shoulder... shots PAST GUN... make Remy the CENTER POINT.

Post-it (bottom right):
133 — Hectic, whip PANS....
DURING STANDOFF
Play shock of TEABING REACTION
TEABING HIT — OUT OF THE BLUE

159

160

to face a spreading group of nuns in habits walking towards him.

Remy shoves through the shocked and PROTESTING women, gun pointing, then slows and finally stops, actually smiling.

Langdon jerks Sophie out of the alley into the moving sea of people.

EXT. LIMO TRUNK – DAY
Teabing doesn't even have time to protest as the trunk is SLAMMED hard over him, leaving him in darkness.

EXT. FLEET STREET – DAY – CONTINUOUS
Sophie and Langdon BANG into people as they continue to run; finally he pulls her into an alcove.

> **LANGDON**
> I don't think he's following.

Both are winded, hands to knees as people pass. Real life, moving by, giving them barely a second glance.

> **SOPHIE**
> What were they? Doves?

Langdon just shakes his head, this oddness lost on neither. Sophie peers out, down the block. Langdon pushes her back into the alcove as a familiar black limo cruises past.

LIMO CLOSER. Not the same car after all. A Sikh in the backseat on a cell phone. Eyes lock; the moment between Sophie and Langdon hangs, then passes.

> **LANGDON**
> They'll keep Leigh alive until they find the Grail.

> **SOPHIE**
> Then we have to find it before they do. But where?

> **LANGDON**
> I need to get to a library.

EXT./INT. CHATEAU VILLETTE – BARN – MORNING
Collet walks with a subordinate.

> **SUBORDINATE**
> **One flag off the prints.**

> **COLLET**
> *(reading)*
> **Remy Legaludec. Petty theft. Skipped out on a hospital bill for an emergency tracheotomy. Peanut allergy.**

They pass a collection of luxury cars.

SUBORDINATE
Yes. And this.

The subordinate gestures towards a ladder. Collet climbs to the unusually clean hay loft above and the AGENT waiting there.

PTS AGENT
Very advanced surveillance.

Nestled against the far wall sits an elaborate work station, CPUs, flat screens, hard drives.

C, A STILL IMAGE OF REMY – LOOKING A LITTLE BIT YOUNGER,

MATCH DISSOLVE TO,

VISUAL EFFECT

INTERPOL

110032-1102

1100

D, PULL BACK TO REVEAL REMY'S MUG SHOT ON COMPUTER SCREEN,

OFFICER 1,
"ONE FLAG OFF THE PRINTS, REMY LEGALDEC, PETTY THEFT."

PULL BACK

E, CONTINUE PULL BACK – REVEALING OFFICER,

OFFICER 1,
"SKIPPED OUT ON A HOSPITAL BILL AFTER AN EMERGENCY TRACHEOTOMY, PEANUT ALLERGY."

PULL BACK

PTS AGENT
It's a listening post.

Collet inspects stacks of labeled mini-disks.

COLLET
Get me Fache.

His expression has grown dark.

COLLET
Four of these names are the men killed last night.

INT. LIMO – ROADSIDE – DAY
Remy drives. He turns to Silas.

REMY
He once whined to me about the wasted space of so large a trunk. Let's see if he complains so now.

SILAS
Are you the Teacher?

REMY
Superbly done. I only regret you had to endure captivity for so long.

SILAS
Physical discomfort has no meaning.

REMY
Of course.

Remy takes a beat.

REMY
You have been of great service.

Storyboards by Robert Ballantyne.

Silas can't help but register his TONE.

> **SILAS**
> The cryptex has yet to be opened. I
> can still serve.

> **REMY**
> You have done enough. The Bishop
> will know of your devotion.

Silas says nothing. Only his eyes convey emotion.

> **REMY**
> I sense disappointment. We cannot let
> ego deter us from our goal.

> **SILAS**
> *(in Spanish)*
> I understand.

Remy pulls the car up to the curb in front of an Opus Dei residence.

> **REMY**
> Good. Wait here in this house of Opus
> Dei and just rewards will soon be
> yours. Bless you, Silas.

Silas bows slightly. That light in his eyes may be tears.

> **SILAS**
> Teacher . . .

Remy kisses his pale forehead.

> **REMY**
> Christ be with you.

INT. SAUNIERE'S LIBRARY – FARMHOUSE – DAY – MOS
Young Sophie is in the corner of the room. Books

lie scattered on the floor. Sauniere stands over her, SHOUTING.

Sophie is SHOUTING back. Shaking her head. He raises his hand, swings to strike . . .

INT. BUS – UPPER LEVEL – MORNING – MOVING (BARELY)
(OVER) A SLAP. Sophie squeezes her eyes shut to block out the memory. The bus inches through grim morning traffic.

> **LANGDON**
> It's going to take forever to get to
> University of London in this traffic.

He is standing beside her, appraising a route map. A police car crawls past. Langdon and Sophie clock it silently.

SERIES OF SHOTS. People: looking at them? A headline: *Murder in the Louvre*. Cocteau's beast grins down from a poster.

LANGDON
Where are you going?

SOPHIE
Getting you a library card.

Langdon watches Sophie cross the bus, TALKING to a YOUTH holding a Treo. Sophie hands him money as Langdon joins her.

SOPHIE
I rented it for you.

She hands him the Treo.

YOUTH
You didn't say you had a boyfriend.

Langdon is starting to familiarize himself with the small device, already working the keys.

LANGDON
I think there's a data base — Here we go. Fast little thing.

As Langdon continues to type, Sophie notices a woman staring at the blood-soaked holes in her stocking knees.

Sophie moves behind an empty seat and, pulling down her skirt, expertly maneuvers out of her panty hose. The youth can't help but notice. Sophie shoos him away with her eyes.

LANGDON
I'm getting all kinds of hits for tombs in London.
(frustrated)
Compounding key words. Knight, London, Pope, Orb.

Now it's Langdon's turn to sneak a look at Sophie. She catches him and throws back a mischievous twinkle.

LANGDON
(typing)
Grail. Rose. Sangreal. Chalice.

YOUTH *(over)*
That ain't going to work, mate.

Langdon looks to him.

> **YOUTH**
> Run a standard Boolean, you should.

> **LANGDON**
> Can you on this?

> **YOUTH**
> I can.

The kid reaches out. Langdon hands him the uplink, the boy now clicking keys with impossible speed.

> **YOUTH**
> Here's your problem, mate. You got a blocking artifact. It's your basic linguistic coincidence. Keywords keep bringing up the writings of some bloke named Alexander Pope.

> **LANGDON**
> Sophie. Your grandfather was a genius.

EXT. WHARF – DAY
Remy looks out at the water. We see only details of the MAN to whom he speaks. Hands. An eye. Half a smile.

> **REMY**
> Sorry about the charade. But I had to improvise, your precious treasure was almost lost. And with it my fortune.

Remy is clearly basking in success.

> **REMY**
> Can you believe how well I did? I even convinced the monk. I should be in theater.

Remy hands over the rose box. In exchange, he takes a silver flask from his companion's gloved hand.

> **REMY**
> A toast to our success, *Teacher*.
> The end of the journey is near.

Remy takes a long swig, too loose from the day's adrenaline.

> **REMY**
> I appreciate the faith you put in me nearly as much as the money, you know. Your identity shall go with me to the grave.

Remy is suddenly hot, loosens his collar. He wipes his forehead, sweat beading on flesh now.

> **TEACHER**
> *(whispered)*
> I know.

Remy's hands clasp at his throat, finally breath going out of the servant, eyes fixed now, wide and sightless.

REMY
Peanuts.

The Teacher's hand reaches into Remy's jacket, finds a cell phone there. Gloved fingers begin to dial.

INT. LONDON POLICE – CAPTAIN'S OFFICE – DAY
A POLICEWOMAN ENTERS the small office where Fache stands TALKING to a British POLICE CAPTAIN.

POLICEWOMAN
We just got a 999 call. Triangulation leads back to the docklands.

She's got their attention.

POLICEWOMAN
Caller was male. Claimed he knew the location of two murderers wanted by French police. He gave us an address.

POLICE CAPTAIN
Send cars.

FACHE
(leaning in)
Did he give their names?

EXT. LONDON – STREET – WALKING
Langdon is leading Sophie down the street.

LANGDON
The knight we're looking for is Sir
Isaac Newton.

*As Langdon CONTINUES, the world around them
transforms to 1727. A regal funeral procession passes.*

LANGDON
His labors produced new sciences
that incurred the wrath of the Church.
Gravity for God's sake.

Langdon and Sophie face the giant stone facade of
Westminster Abbey. *The FUNERAL PROCESSION
heads inside the church.*

LANGDON
And, if you chose to believe, a Grand
Master of the Priory as well.

TRACK WITH LANGDON & SOPHIE

christopher glass '04

LANGDON CONT'D: "... THAT INCURRED THE WRATH OF THE CHURCH..."
VERY SUBTLEY EARLY 18th CENTURY "SOLDIERS" ARE MIXED IN
WITH THE MODERN CROWDED LONDON STREETS. THE CAMERA DOESN'T
ATTEMPT TO DRAW ATTENTION TO THEM. (THEY DON'T "APPEAR" - THEY ARE
ALREADY THERE)

Storyboard by Christopher Glass.

Lincoln as Westminster

A major location challenge was the transformation of Lincoln Cathedral into Westminster Abbey. Lincoln was chosen to stand in for Westminster based on its very similar interior architecture, including its own Chapter House. It lacked an important element, however—the famous tomb of Sir Isaac Newton, which would serve as a centerpiece of the scene.

OPPOSITE: Three views of Lincoln Cathedral used for filming key scenes: the Chapter House (below), the Nave (above left), and the Cloisters (above right). ABOVE: Exterior of Westminster Abbey in London. BELOW: Star power: Ron Howard, Tom Hanks, Audrey Tautou, Jean Reno, Ian McKellen, and Brian Grazer outside Westminster Abbey.

TRACK

christopher glass '04

LANGDON CONT'D : " ... GRAVITY FOR GOD'S SAKE."

MORE 18TH CENTURY PARTICIPANTS IN A FUNERAL PROCESSION
ARE IN THE SHOT - MIXED WITH MODERN LONDON. AGAIN,
THEY ARE "MATTER-OF-FACTLY" IN THE SHOT.

CAMERA CRANES TO REVEAL:

christopher glass '04.

FUNERAL

LANGDON & SOPHIE

FUNERAL

1727 - SIR ISAAC NEWTON'S FUNERAL
LANGDON & SOPHIE WALK WITH PROCESSION

INT. WESTMINSTER ABBEY – CONTINUOUS
Resplendent. Sophie and Langdon walk up the aisle,
pews filled with elegant mourners of three centuries ago.

                    SOPHIE
        But if he offended the Catholic
        Church, the Pope would be the last
        person to preside over his funeral.

                    LANGDON
        That's where I got it wrong. In London
        lies a knight *A* pope interred.

Langdon points to *the pulpit where a MAN stands, giving a sermon, his VOICE an echo across the centuries.*

                    LANGDON
        Sir Isaac Newton's burial was pre-
        sided over by his friend and colleague
        Alexander Pope.

Langdon looks at Sophie *as the world of the past vanishes,*
the present-day church already greeting its first visitors.

                    LANGDON
        A pope. His first initial. How did I
        miss that?

Sophie stops before a massive black marble sarcophagus. Nearby stacked boards and plaster signal ongoing
renovation.

*OPPOSITE: Storyboards by Christopher Glass. ABOVE: Visual effects and practical location merge past
and present versions of Westminster Abbey, in order to reinforce the past's bearing on the present.*

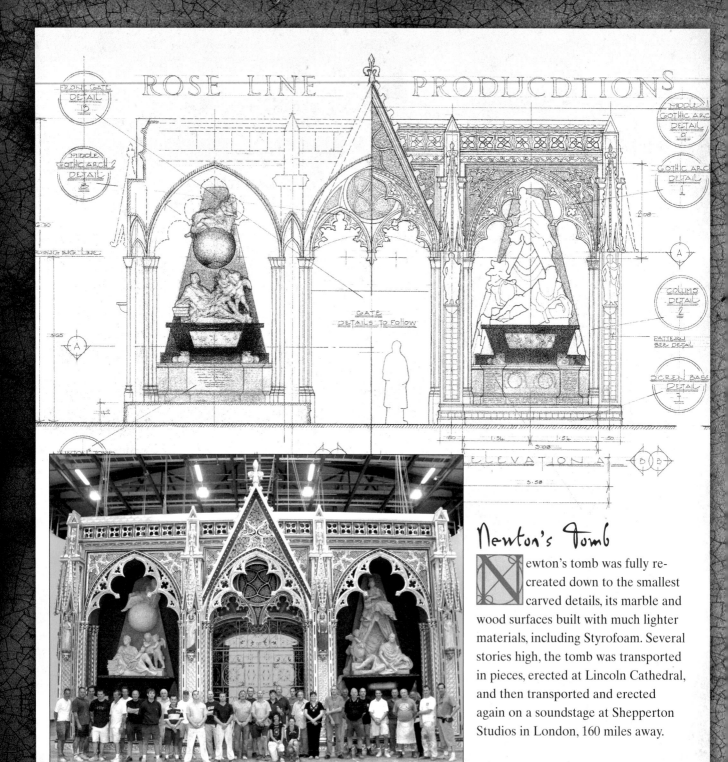

Newton's Tomb

Newton's tomb was fully re-created down to the smallest carved details, its marble and wood surfaces built with much lighter materials, including Styrofoam. Several stories high, the tomb was transported in pieces, erected at Lincoln Cathedral, and then transported and erected again on a soundstage at Shepperton Studios in London, 160 miles away.

SOPHIE

Here.

Langdon touches a reclining sculpture of Newton on the tomb. Behind him is a pyramid, on which a giant circle is mounted.

SOPHIE

An orb.

LANGDON

Not just one.

Langdon looks closer. On the orb itself, carved in bas-relief, a myriad of heavenly bodies. All circular.

LANGDON

There's no way to tell if any orb in particular is missing.

SOPHIE

An orb with rosy flesh and seeded womb?

LANGDON

These are planets. Constellations. Signs of the zodiac . . .

But she's not paying attention. She's staring at trodden shapes in the plaster dust at their feet.

Ghost Remy and Ghost Silas escort Ghost Teabing towards the tomb.

SOPHIE

Robert, these tracks. Look at the cane marks. Were they here already?

Ghost Remy and Ghost Silas vanish, Ghost Teabing now standing alone.

SOPHIE
(crouching)
But there are no other footprints. . . .
He was alone.

VOICE (over)

I'm sorry.

A FIGURE emerges from behind the tomb. Teabing himself.

TEABING

You were never to be a part of this, Robert. But when you two arrived at my home as you did, others might call it God's will.

Passing tourists pay them little attention.

TEABING

I believed if I had the cryptex I could solve the riddle alone. I was . . . unworthy.

He looks at Sophie.

TEABING

But you. You are here for a reason. You are the last remaining guardian of the Grail. Your grandfather and the other *sénéchaux* would not have lied with dying breath unless they knew their secret was preserved.

SOPHIE

How could you know Sauniere's last words?

LANGDON

Oh, Leigh.

TEABING

Grail quests require sacrifice.

SOPHIE

Murderer.

TEABING

No, no. Tell her, Robert. Murderers are heroes when history is written.

SOPHIE

You self-righteous bastard.

LANGDON

Sophie, walk away.

TEABING

Don't! Don't. I'll do what I have to now. Anything.

Teabing shows something in his hand. A gun.

TEABING

Please. Do you understand?

He CLICKS back the hammer, gestures with his hidden gun.

TEABING

Now, can't we all be friends again? This way.

INT. OPUS DEI HOUSE – RESIDENCE – KENSINGTON
Similar to that room in Paris. Silas rises from the floor, his back bloody from a fresh and savage whipping.

The monk freezes, distracted by something. Then Silas, naked, crosses to the window.

Through a hedge, the outline of a car pulling up. On its roof, a bar of police lights.

INT. OPUS DEI HOUSE – HALLWAY
Still pulling on his robes, Silas emerges from his room, moving quietly. Gun drawn, he glances down the stairwell.

Police are gathering in the foyer, talking to the desk-man.

(OVER) A SHOUT. Silas spins. A cop stands at the end of the hall, begins chase. Silas sprints down the service stairs.

EXT. OPUS DEI HOUSE – STREET – CONTINUOUS
PAN OFF more cop cars spilling cops to see Aringarosa coming down the street in the background.

Exploding out the service door, Silas doesn't see the waiting COP; their bodies collide.

Behind, more COPS (OVER) coming out of the open door. Rolling, Silas FIRES as the officers emerge.

BANG! Silas grabs the sudden red wound in his shoulder. Stumbling up, he spins, FIRING, cops' blood spraying.

A dark shadow looms behind him from nowhere.

> **VOICE**
> Silas! Stop!

Silas spins and FIRES. His eyes meet his victim's as the man falls. Aringarosa drops, blood running out of him, his briefcase spilling hundreds of bearer bonds on the wind.

> **ARINGAROSA**
> I am sorry, son. We are betrayed.

Silas cradles Aringarosa, stares down in horror. SHOUTS. More cops converging. A beat.

> **SILAS**
> *(in Spanish)*
> I am a ghost.

Silas simply aims his gun. They FIRE.

EXT. WESTMINSTER COURTYARD – DAY
Teabing guides them through a courtyard that abuts
a structure with a hanging sign: CLOSED FOR
RENOVATION.

> **TEABING**
> I'm going to put this gun down. I only
> want you both to listen.

He's walking behind them. People cross the cloister
towards them, LAUGHING, from the other direction.

> **TEABING**
> A few moments, Robert, and I'll put this away.

> **LANGDON**
> We're listening, Leigh.

> **TEABING**
> For 2,000 years the Church has rained
> oppression and atrocity upon mankind,
> crushed passion and idea alike with their
> stranglehold on society, all in the name of
> their walking God.

Langdon clocks the people as they close. Considering.

> **TEABING**
> Proof of Jesus' mortality can bring
> an end to all that suffering, drive this
> church of lies to its knees. The living
> heir must be revealed. Jesus must be
> shown for what he was, not miraculous,
> simply man.

Langdon lets the people pass, unaware.

TEABING
The dark con can be exposed.
Mankind can finally be set free.

Teabing gestures them into the abandoned wing.

TEABING
We can do it, Robert. The three of us.
We can set the world free.

EXT. OPUS DEI HOUSE – STREET – DAY
Cops are gathering up colorful banknotes. Aringarosa is being moved towards an ambulance.

A figure stops the medics. Fache. He looks down at the Bishop, the clergyman's lips red with bubbling blood.

ARINGAROSA
How is Silas? Will he live?

FACHE
The monk?

Aringarosa manages a nod.

FACHE
Bishop, how would you know this killer's name?

ARINGAROSA
Help me get away from here, Fache.

FACHE
This monk who kills with such ease?
Who just arrived from France?

Fache's expression darkens, pieces now falling into place.

FACHE
Langdon never came to you in confession, did he?

ARINGAROSA
You see the money. There's more, understand? I can't be implicated. There are still
important works to be done.

FACHE
You used me.

ARINGAROSA
God uses us all.

Fache reaches into Aringarosa's bloody jacket, the
Bishop capable of only feeble resistance, and finds
a cell phone.

FACHE
(to a cop)
I need a trace. Quickly.

He turns back to the Bishop.

FACHE
Your Silas is dead.

INT. WESTMINSTER ABBEY – ABANDONED WING
Scaffolding and slatted sunlight. Plaster dust twirls in
small dervishes on the ancient stone floors. Teabing
urges them forward, gun coming fully visible.

TEABING
The Priory failed their sacred charge.
The millennium came and went and
the heir remained hidden. What choice
did I have?

Teabing sweeps a worktable clear.

Script Page 1 (Sunflower Yellow Revisions):

Sunflower Yellow Revisions 16/08/05 125.

148   CONTINUED: 148

He turns back to the Bishop.

           FACHE
      Your Silas is dead.

149   INT. WESTMINSTER ABBEY - ABANDONED WING   149

Scaffolding and slatted sunlight. Plaster dust twirls in
small dervishes on the ancient stone floors.

           TEABING
      The Priory failed their sacred
      charge. The millennium came and
      went and the heir remained hidden.
      What choice did I have?

Through the despotism in his eyes, real sadness.

           TEABING
      I sought out the enemy. I persuaded
      the Council of Shadows I was their
      ally.

He shakes his head.

           TEABING
      Rhetor, I made them call me
      Teacher. I schooled them in grace.
      And sacrifice.

He has turned now, eyes fixed on Sophie.

           TEABING
      You are my miracle, Sophie. All the
      oppression of the poor and
      powerless, of those of different
      skin, of women. Fiery eternal
      damnation for those who do not
      believe as the church believes. You
      can end all that. Your grandfather
      left you the key for a reason. You
      must explode the truth onto the
      world. It is your duty.

Teabing lifts the cryptex.

           TEABING
      You are the last of the Senechaux.
      You know this riddle's key. Tell me
      how to open this and I'll put the
      gun down. Together we can begin to
      right centuries of terrible wrongs.

Script Page 2 (Emerald Green Revisions):

148   CONTINUED: *Emerald Green Revisions 16/08/05* 125.   148

He turns back to the Bishop.

           FACHE
      Your Silas is dead.

149   INT. WESTMINSTER ABBEY - ABANDONED WING   149

Scaffolding and slatted sunlight. Plaster dust twirls in
small dervishes on the ancient stone floors. Teabing urges
them forward, gun coming fully visible.

           TEABING
      The Priory failed their sacred
      charge. The millennium came and
      went and the heir remained hidden.
      What choice did I have?

Through the despotism in his eyes, real sadness.

           TEABING
      I sought out the enemy. I persuaded
      the Council of Shadows I was their
      ally.

He shakes his head.

           TEABING
      Rhetor, I made them call me
      Teacher. I schooled them in grace.
      And sacrifice. On your knees. Do
      it.

He has positioned himself against a work table. Gun waving,
they have no choice but to oblige.

           TEABING
      You are my miracle, Sophie. All the
      oppression of the poor and
      powerless, of those of different
      skin, of women. You can end all
      that. Your grandfather left you the
      key for a reason. You must explode
      the truth onto the world. It is
      your duty.

Teabing rolls the cryptex gently across the floor and it
settles in front of them.

           TEABING
      You are the last of the Senechaux.
      You know the answer to this riddle.
           (MORE)

Script Page 3 (Sorbet Goldenrod Revisions):

Sorbet Goldenrod Revisions 17/08/05 125. 148

148   CONTINUED:

He turns back to the Bishop.
           FACHE
      Your Silas is dead.   149

149   INT. WESTMINSTER ABBEY - ABANDONED WING

Scaffolding and slatted sunlight. Plaster dust twirls in
small dervishes on the ancient stone floors. Teabing urges
them forward, gun coming fully visible.

           TEABING
      The Priory failed their sacred
      charge. The millennium came and
      went and the heir remained hidden.
      What choice did I have?

Teabing sweeps a work table clear.

           TEABING
      I sought out the enemy. I persuaded
      the Council of Shadows I was their
      ally.

He shakes his head.

           TEABING
      Rhetor, I made them call me
      Teacher. I schooled them in grace.
      And sacrifice.

           LANGDON
      Leigh, can we just—

           TEABING
      Robert, get down. On your knees. Do
      it.

He has positioned himself against the table. Gun waving,
Langdon has no choice but to oblige. Sophie begins to kneel
as well.

           TEABING
      Not you, my dear. You are my
      miracle, Sophie. All the oppression
      of the poor and powerless, of those
      of different skin, of women. You
      can end all that. Your grandfather
      left you the key for a reason. You
      must explode the truth onto the
      world. It is your duty.

Evolution of Dialogue

Script dialogue evolves over many drafts and many months. In this scene, the final confrontation between Langdon, Sophie, and Teabing, the script changed during rehearsal, the day before shooting, and the day of the shoot—right up to the moment when the cameras rolled.

TEABING

I sought out the enemy. I persuaded the
Council of Shadows I was their ally.

He shakes his head.

TEABING

Rhetor, I made them call me. Teacher. I
schooled them in grace. And sacrifice.

LANGDON

Leigh, can we just —

TEABING

Robert, get down. On your knees. Do it.

He has positioned himself against the table, gun waving.
Langdon has no choice but to oblige. Sophie begins to
kneel as well.

TEABING

Not you, my dear. You are my miracle,
Sophie. All the oppression of the poor
and powerless, of those of different
skin, of women. You can end all that.
Your grandfather left you the key for
a reason. You must explode the truth
onto the world. It is your duty.

Teabing rolls the cryptex gently across the floor and it
settles in front of them.

TEABING

You are the last of the *sénéchaux*.
You know the answer to this riddle.
Open the cryptex and I'll throw
away the gun.

Sophie stares at him a beat.

SOPHIE

I have no idea how. And even if I did, I
wouldn't tell you.

Sophie kneels. Teabing begins moving across the room.

TEABING

So like your grandfather, then. Willing
to die for your secret.

He slips around behind them.

TEABING

But by the way you've been looking at
your hero, I wonder, would you let him
die for you?

Teabing raises his gun to Langdon's head.

TEABING

Open it, Sophie. To save his life.

LANGDON

Leigh —

TEABING
Open the cryptex.

Her response isn't to Teabing but to Langdon.

SOPHIE
I don't know how —

TEABING
Open it or he dies —

SOPHIE
I swear. I don't know —

LANGDON
Stop! Both of you. Stop.

He's got their attention.

LANGDON
She can't do it, Leigh. But maybe . . .
Give me a second.

A long beat, then Teabing shifts the gun to Sophie's head. Langdon lifts the cryptex.

Langdon rises. Teabing cocks the gun.

Langdon starts across the room.

TEABING
What are you doing —

LANGDON
Shh, shh, shh.

Newton's tomb begins to form in the air, ghostly but present.

The constellations begin to move, slowly twirling around him.

Then the planets join the stars.

Then the signs of the zodiac, all in a celestial waltz.

Langdon stands in the center of this spinning dance of impossible beauty.

Now the orbs begin whipping away, one by one.

More and more orbs are rejected, violently hurling back into the tomb's face, ever fewer now swinging around Langdon.

Finally, a flurry of exits until only one orb spins, not really an orb at all, but a small globe of negative space.

That single negative orb freezes, turns red and shiny.

And winks out.

Langdon stands with his back to Teabing and Sophie a beat, his hands unseen. Finally he drops his head in despair.

LANGDON
(turning to Sophie)
I'm sorry.

Now he looks to his old friend, his tone suddenly defiant.

LANGDON
I'm sorry.

Langdon launches the cryptex up towards the ceiling.

TEABING
No!

Teabing reacts on instinct. He releases his gun, crutch dropping, stretching arms grabbing the keystone in midair.

But Teabing is falling too fast. His outstretched arms hit first, gun going off. (OVER) A CRUNCH as the cryptex hits the floor.

TEABING
Robert, no, fool.

Teabing is tearing off the top of the cryptex, vinegar flowing through his trembling fingers.

                    TEABING
          The map is ruined. The Grail is lost.
          The Grail!

                    LANGDON
          Only the worthy find the Grail, Leigh.

The DOORS swing open. Bezu Fache, followed by several British police.

                    FACHE
          That one. The old man.

Fache pulls the cell phone from Teabing's pocket. The cops pull Teabing up roughly, already beginning to plastic cuff him.

                    FACHE
          Cell phones are quite simple to locate these days.

INT. WESTMINSTER ABBEY – RECTORY OFFICE – DAY
Shafts of light illuminate Sophie, blanket around her
shoulders as she inspects a steaming cup of tea.

Langdon sits beside her, hand on her knee, staring at
a wooden desk adorned with the bagged anatomy of a
crime.

A COP stands not far off, silent. Fache stands in the
doorway with his aide, TALKING. Both ENTER.

> FACHE
> Big crowd out there now.

His eyes are as haunted as Langdon's and Sophie's as he
comes around to the other side of the desk.

> FACHE
> Thank you for your statements. You
> are free to go, of course.

But Langdon just keeps staring at the evidence. Cryptex.
Rose box. Gun. Canes. Corpse photos. Cash. Cell phone.

> FACHE
> **Leave us, please.**

The cops walk out the door. Fache sits, watches
them go.

> FACHE
> I should have been smarter.

Fache's smile is wan.

> FACHE
> **I acted on faith, I suppose.**

> SOPHIE
> *(off the photos)*
> How many?

Fache understands, just shrugs.

> FACHE
> Your grandfather. The other three.
> Maybe more. The monk was given
> to him as a gift, it seems. To do as he
> asked. He used him well before send-
> ing him to slaughter.

Sophie's eyes register the news.

> FACHE
> He killed the servant himself, you
> know?

> SOPHIE
> Remy?

> FACHE
> By poison.

Fache has slid the bagged flask towards them. Langdon
turns it over in his hand.

> SOPHIE
> And us. He told Remy to kill us.

Langdon closes his eyes; endless ringing betrayal.

> FACHE
> You believed he was your friend. We
> can only act according to our beliefs. It
> is our nature.

Not just talking about Langdon. A matched pair, these
men.

LANGDON
How much of it have you put together?

FACHE
Some. Not enough for it to make sense.

SOPHIE
It won't ever make sense.

No argument there. Fache stands. Extends his hand.

FACHE
I am sorry.

Langdon accepts his grasp.

LANGDON
Yeah.

Fache leads towards the door. But Langdon has paused over Teabing's canes. Sophie hangs back with him a beat.

LANGDON
He forgot everything we learn.
Everything we teach.

So much loss in his eyes. And sadness.

LANGDON
It's why we study history. So we stop
killing each other.

She touches his arm. They head towards the outside light.

EXT. WESTMINSTER ABBEY – DAY – MINUTES LATER
Police cars are parked at raking angles. Sophie and Langdon stand across the street as two cops emerge,

carrying Teabing under the arms. Leigh turns to look at Langdon.

> **TEABING**
>
> How could you do it, Robert? To destroy our hope for freedom. To deny every pilgrim the chance to kneel at the tomb of the Magdalen. How could you —

That's when Teabing's eyes change. That old sparkle.

> **TEABING**
>
> You couldn't. You solved it. You took out the scroll before it broke. You solved it.

His eyes are on fire, head craning as he is brought to the car.

> **TEABING**
>
> You'll find it, Robert. You'll find it. You know what to do. Find the Grail. Kneel before her. Set her free upon the world.

The cops are putting him in the backseat. Fache separates from the British captain, walks to Sophie and Langdon.

> **TEABING**
>
> The map to the Holy Grail. He has it. The Holy Grail.

The door SLAMS. Fache holds Langdon's eyes.

> **FACHE**
>
> Mad, I suppose.

LANGDON

Or worse.

FACHE

**I am relieved neither of you were hurt,
Agent Neveu.**

SOPHIE

**I think today was the first time I've
ever been happy to see you.**

Fache chuckles. (OVER) A cop SHOUTS for him.
Fache switches back to English.

FACHE

The British have no idea how to run
an investigation. Excuse me.

Then Fache simply nods and heads down the steps,
towards his waiting aide. Sophie and Langdon watch
him go.

LANGDON

He was right, of course. It was actually
pretty easy.

Langdon opens his palm to show a narrow scroll of
papyrus.

LANGDON

There was every conceivable orb on that
tomb, except one. The orb that fell from
the heavens and inspired Newton's life's
work. Work that incurred the wrath of the
Church until his dying day.

SOPHIE

. . . His labor's fruit. The rosy flesh with
seeded womb.

LANGDON

That orb from which Eve herself par-
took. A.P.P.L.E. Apple.

He unrolls the small parchment.

LANGDON

*The Holy Grail 'neath ancient Roslin waits.
The blade and chalice guarding o'er Her
gates. Adorned in masters' loving art, She
lies. She rests at last beneath the starry skies.*

Langdon looks up at her.

LANGDON

I think I know where she's gone. I
think the Grail has gone home.

**EXT. WINDING ROAD – ROSSLYN, SCOTLAND – LATE
DAY**

A rented car winds up towards a hilltop church.

EXT. ROSSLYN CHAPEL – PARKING AREA – LATE DAY

Langdon and Sophie emerge from the car. They stare up
at the stark edifice framed against glowing clouds.

LANGDON

Rosslyn Chapel. Built by the Templars.
In 1446. It sits directly on the original
rose line.

EXT. ROSSLYN CHAPEL LAWN – CONTINUOUS

Sophie and Langdon cross the green towards the main
doors.

LANGDON

The Holy Grail, 'neath ancient Roslin waits . . .

SOPHIE

So this is it. The gift at the end?

Langdon shakes his head. He doesn't know for sure.

SOPHIE
You never told me. The joke Sauniere made of you. What was it?

LANGDON
He called me a flatfoot. A beat cop of history.

He misunderstands her smile, keeps explaining.

LANGDON
A dumb policeman — who just does his job day after day — of history.

Sophie's LAUGH is unexpected.

SOPHIE
You know his father was one. A policeman.

Langdon just shakes his head.

SOPHIE
Sauniere said he was the most honorable man he had ever known.

Langdon is speechless.

SOPHIE
We are who we protect, I think. What we stand up for.

They have come to the old wooden door. They push inside.

©Brad Braun

Rosslyn: Real and Reimagined

Filming in a six-hundred-year-old building presents unique challenges. Rosslyn Chapel is enshrouded in rich history . . . as well as in a maze of restorative scaffolding that covers much of its exterior surface. Initially the plan was to shoot the exterior and digitally erase the scaffolding in post-production. A far more practical solution was found, however, when VFX producer Barrie Hemsley commissioned the construction of a one-sixth scale model of the chapel. This was filmed as a stand-alone element, which was composited into the live-action shots caught on location.

INT. ROSSLYN CHAPEL – MAGIC HOUR

Late sun draws geometries of dust in the air. Langdon stares up at a ceiling densely carved with symbols.

> **LANGDON**
> Jewish, Christian, Egyptian, Masonic, pagan . . .

But Sophie's not listening. She's stopped, turning now, in the center of the shadowy space around her.

> **SOPHIE**
> I think . . . I was here before.

Heading towards the door, Sophie sees the ghosts of a LAUGHING couple leaving, a little boy between them.

> **GHOST SOPHIE'S MOTHER**
> Sophie.

Sophie's smaller self races past to join waiting parents.

> **SOPHIE**
> A very long time ago.

The girl turns. Young Sophie holds Sophie's eyes a beat across time. Then she turns away, into the light and gone.

> **VOICE**
> On a Grail quest, I assume?

Langdon and Sophie start. A DOCENT has come beside them.

> **DOCENT**
> Sorry. The cup was rumored to be hidden here once. That's why people come, mostly. And a few to pray.

LANGDON
The symbol for male . . .

The upright triangle on the symbol glows for a moment.

LANGDON
And female.

Now the lower triangle glows.

SOPHIE
Fused as one.

LANGDON
As the pagans would have wanted.

The docent sees Langdon already moving towards the stair.

DOCENT
We're about to close, I'm afraid . . .

LANGDON
We'll just be a second.

He drops a few euros in the collection box and heads down the ancient steps.

SOPHIE
You're not still telling people it's a cup?

Langdon smiles.

LANGDON
Inverted and right triangles. Pagan symbols for man and woman.

DOCENT
Well, I'm sure you'll find no few of those overhead. Happy hunting.

The docent has already moved away.

LANGDON
Not on the ceiling. Over there.

Langdon is pointing towards a descending stair over which a single symbol is emblazoned.

SOPHIE
The blade and chalice guard her gates.

INT. ROSSLYN CHAPEL – LOWER LEVEL – MAGIC HOUR
Cement walls older than most spoken languages.

> **LANGDON**
> Wow.

Sophie follows him in. Langdon's looking for something. They move through a small side chamber into . . .

INT. ROSSLYN CHAPEL – STORAGE ROOM – MAGIC HOUR
Old. And crowded. Full of nonsecular statuary, boxes of old documents, cases of candles, two crèches. No floor space. The walls are ringed with old paintings. Langdon's eyes narrow.

> **LANGDON**
> I've never seen these before. But the style is unmistakable. Leonardo Da Vinci.

He indicates two particular paintings hanging directly across from each other on opposite walls.

INT. ROSSLYN CHAPEL – SMALL CHAMBER – CONTINUOUS
The docent stands just outside the large room. Listening.

> **LANGDON** (over)
> *Adorned in masters' loving art she lies.*

Something changes in the docent's eyes. He steps away.

INT. ROSSLYN CHAPEL – STORAGE ROOM – CONTINUOUS
Sophie is staring up. Overhead, the vaulted ceiling is peppered, in no perceptible pattern, with pentagrams.

SOPHIE
She rests at last beneath starry skies.

Sophie moves to a spot where a peppered star overhead falls on the line between the two paintings.

She lifts an old carpet directly below bearing a crescent moon. A circular handle is cut flush into the floor. On it, an engraved fleur-de-lis. She and Langdon exchange a look.

He pulls. Below is a stairway hardly big enough for one.

LANGDON
What is it with today?

EXT. ROSSYLN CHAPEL – MAGIC HOUR
The docent stands at the door as a car pulls up. Two men emerge. Another car can be seen closing in the distance.

INT. ROSSLYN CHAPEL – HIDDEN STAIRCASE – CONTINUOUS
Langdon breezes through the tight space. Surprised at the ease with which he descends wet stone steps. Below, light, brighter as they approach until they come to an archway.

INT. ROSSLYN CHAPEL – SECRET LIBRARY – CONTINUOUS
Lit by afternoon light coming through strategically placed vents. Here, shelves of far older books, scrolls and parchments.

SOPHIE
She was here.

Sophie is inspecting an outline on the floor in the center of the room; a heavy object once stood here a long time. And it was human shaped.

SOPHIE
How was I ever supposed to figure all this out?

But Langdon isn't listening. He's gathered and opened several vellum bags, now examining newspaper articles.

LANGDON
What was it about, Sophie? When you and your grandfather fought.

As he turns to look at her, his expression is different.

LANGDON
Was it something about your past? About how your family died?

SOPHIE
How could you know that?

He just stares at her. When she finally speaks, *the walls fade away.*

SOPHIE
It was during primary school. I was in his library. Doing research.

LANGDON
A sarcophagus.

SOPHIE
Mary Magdalen.

LANGDON
The Holy Grail.

SOPHIE
Where did she go? Did the Church finally get her?

But Langdon is examining one of the bookshelves.

LANGDON
These records date back to the death of Christ.

EXT. ROSSYLN CHAPEL – MAGIC HOUR
Maybe ten cars. The last men and women are heading into the church. The docent BOLTS the door shut.

INT. ROSSYLN CHAPEL – SECRET LIBRARY – MAGIC HOUR
Sophie explores cases with shelves bearing the names of the Grand Masters. Newton. Hugo. Debussy. Cocteau.

Creating a Life History

The details of Sophie's past are imagined in newspaper articles from around the globe.

Young Sophie from the opening, poring over books.

SOPHIE
I wanted to know about them. But I
couldn't find any records. Not of their
death. Not of the accident.

Sauniere storms into the room.

SOPHIE
He was always such a gentle man. He
started shouting at me. I shouted back.
And he hit me, Robert.

Sauniere towers over his frightened granddaughter.

SOPHIE
He stood over me and wouldn't let
me leave. Not until he made me swear
never to try to find out what happened
to them.

*Young Sophie from the opening, holding our gaze in
confused angry eyes, turns, races away across the field.
Sauniere stares after her in the doorway. HOLD on his
face, so sad.*

SOPHIE
I kept my promise. The next week he
sent me to boarding school. We hardly
ever spoke again.

The wall is closed now, the past gone once more. Sophie
is having trouble keeping her emotions at bay.

LANGDON
Do you have any memories of your
grandfather before the accident?
Before your parents were killed?

SOPHIE
Yes. No. I don't know. Why?

LANGDON
Because I don't think he was your grandfather.

She has come around to where Robert has spread out
several newspaper articles in several languages. See the
headlines: FAMILY KILLED.

SOPHIE
These are my parents. My brother. I
had pictures once.

CLOSE on a newspaper photo of a smiling couple with
two kids. Sophie is nearly overcome by the past and its loss.

LANGDON
And this is you, isn't it?

Langdon points to a small face. Young Sophie.

LANGDON
The entire family was killed, father,
mother, and *both* children: a boy, six,
and a girl, four.

He is reading the text now.

LANGDON
Only your name isn't Sauniere. It's Saint-
Clair. One of the oldest families in France.
From a line of Merovingian kings.

SOPHIE
Quoi?

That's when Langdon turns, shows her the shelves from
where he's taken these documents. On each, a simple
cup and two words: *sang real.*

SOPHIE

Sang real.

LANGDON

Royal blood. I was wrong. Sauniere didn't want you to guard the secret of the Holy Grail. Sophie, you are the secret.

She just stares at him.

LANGDON

You must have survived the accident. If it even was an accident. The Priory found out. They must have concealed the fact that you weren't dead. Hid you with the Grand Master himself, who raised you as his own.

SOPHIE

Non.

LANGDON

According to these. Princess Sophie —

SOPHIE

C'est pas possible.

LANGDON

You are the heir. The end of the blood-line. You are the last living descendant of Jesus Christ.

She stares at him.

SOPHIE

. . . Non.

Sophie puts her back against the wall, sliding down to sit on the floor. Langdon stands over her in fading light.

INT. ROSSYLN CHAPEL – SANCTUARY – MOMENTS LATER
Langdon and Sophie emerge to face maybe twenty people, men and women, old and young, all standing, staring
at them. All staring at Sophie.

> **LANGDON**
> Hello . . . ?

Langdon moves beside her protectively.

> **WOMAN'S VOICE** (over)
> Sophie.

An OLD WOMAN steps forward. She smiles.

> **LANGDON**
> Who are you?

But she's looking only at Sophie.

> **OLD WOMAN**
> There have been many names. The
> keepers. Guardians. The Priory.

Only now does Langdon see, all wear the same pin, a
tiny fleur-de-lis.

> **OLD WOMAN**
> But to you, they are the friends of the
> man who raised you, Jacques Sauniere.

The old woman reaches out and touches Sophie's face.

> **OLD WOMAN**
> He would have wanted you to know.
> That he loved you very much.

Her smile is tender.

OLD WOMAN
And that they are here to protect you now.
As they have always protected our family.

Her eyes hold on to Sophie and then are far away, lost in the past.

OLD WOMAN
I gave you up once, knowing that I
might never see you again.

Eyes sparkling with tears.

OLD WOMAN
So you could live.

Sophie's stare is wide with wonder.

OLD WOMAN
I am your grandmother, Sophie. And
I have prayed for this moment for a
very long time.

The others all bow their heads now, only slightly.

OLD WOMAN
Welcome home, child.

EXT. ROSSYLN CASTLE – MAGIC HOUR
Langdon stands at the edge of a nearby castle. The chapel is visible in the near distance.

SOPHIE
Hey.

Sophie is walking out of the building towards him.

SOPHIE
No more strings.

She moves her wrists freely.

SOPHIE
His last breath. To keep me safe.

She gestures behind her where a few men and women from the church now watch her like parents before a first date.

SOPHIE
She has some things she wants to tell
me. About my family.

Langdon throws a wave.

LANGDON
Hi.

He and Sophie begin to walk up the gravel path.

LANGDON
What will you do?

She just shakes her head. She doesn't know.

LANGDON
The legend will be revealed when the
heir reveals himself.

SOPHIE
They just got the pronoun wrong.

Langdon nods.

SOPHIE
She said when Sauniere died, he took the location of Mary's sarcophagus with him. So there's no way to empirically prove we're related to her.

LANGDON
You sounded just like an academic.

SOPHIE
And even if I was sure . . . How many Catholics in the world? What's more important, Robert? Where faith comes from? Or faith itself?

LANGDON
The only thing that matters is what you believe.

SOPHIE
No more teacher and student.

They have stopped just opposite a small pond. Langdon sits on an old stone fence overlooking worlds of forest below.

LANGDON
History shows Jesus Christ was an extraordinary man. A human inspiration. Just that. That is all the evidence proves.

She nods. But Langdon isn't finished.

LANGDON
But when I was a boy. When I was drowning in that well Teabing told you about. I thought I was going to die, Sophie. And what I did, I prayed. I prayed to Jesus to keep me alive so I could see my parents again, so I could go to school again, so I could play with my dog. I prayed for somebody to find me. And they did. My prayer was answered. And to this day I believe I wasn't alone down there.

She stares at him.

LANGDON
Why couldn't Jesus have been both the Son of God and a man? Why couldn't he be a father and still be capable of all those miracles?

SOPHIE
Like turning water into wine?

Langdon takes a beat before answering.

LANGDON
Who knows? His blood is your blood.

Maybe that junkie in the park will never touch a drug again. Maybe you healed my fear with your hands. Maybe there was no gas in that gas tank after all.

Langdon smiles.

> **LANGDON**
> Why is it always human or divine? Maybe human is divine. One thing I do know. A living heir to Jesus Christ; would she destroy faith? Or would she renew it?

He holds her eyes. Those beautiful eyes. He stands, begins walking with her towards the waiting rental car.

> **LANGDON**
> So I say again. What really matters is what you believe.

> **SOPHIE**
> Thank you. For bringing me here. For letting him choose you. Sir Robert.

Langdon smiles.

> **LANGDON**
> I'm always around if you need me, Sophie.

> **SOPHIE**
> I know.

He leans in and kisses her on the head and she pushes into him, so hard; he holds her close.

> **LANGDON**
> You take care.

Sophie turns. Langdon stands, finding his keys.

> **SOPHIE**
> Hey.

He looks up. She has gone back to that pond. Now she puts her foot on the surface of the water. A beat. It sinks.

> **SOPHIE**
> Nope.

Langdon LAUGHS.

> **SOPHIE**
> Maybe I'll do better with the wine.

She smiles, so warm, and now turns, already heading towards the glowing windows and the safety of a new home.

> **LANGDON**
> Godspeed.

INT. RITZ HOTEL – BATHROOM – NIGHT
Langdon stands at the sink, shirtless, shaving. Razor nicks flesh, quick and deep.

> **LANGDON**
> Damn.

Shakes off that drop of blood, fixes on the sink as red runs down white porcelain, a long thin line. The color of a rose.

INT. RITZ HOTEL – SUITE – NIGHT
TRACK PAST open bags nearly packed, PAST a television, Collet TALKING to an INTERVIEWER on screen.

> **COLLET**
> **Captain Fache seldom makes mistakes. His**

> **manhunt for Agent Neveu and Mr. Langdon was a ruse to lure out the real killer.**

FIND Langdon, still shirtless, standing over an open copy of his new book, rifling pages.

> **COLLET** (*over*)
> **Whether or not Mr. Langdon and Agent Neveu were willing participants in the sting, I do not know . . .**

PAGE – CLOSE. An illustration of lay lines, a linear tapestry. A single line amid the others is adorned with roses beside a single word: ROSELINE. This is the very same page that Sauniere's copy was open to in his office.

> **LANGDON**
> It hides beneath the rose.

EXT. RITZ HOTEL – NIGHT
Langdon, dressed, hurries down the street. Embedded in the pavement, bronze medallions form a perfectly straight line.

EXT. PARIS – STREETS – NIGHT
He follows the markers of the rose line, carefully at first, but as they lead him south, his pace quickens.

> **SAUNIERE'S VOICE** *(over)*
> *The Holy Grail 'neath ancient Rosslyn waits . . .*

He's running now, through the Passage Richelieu, opening tunnel mouth REVEALING . . .

EXT. LOUVRE MUSEUM – NIGHT
Back where all this began. He crosses the grassy Carrousel du Louvre, heading straight for the mighty Pyramide Inversée.

> **SAUNIERE'S VOICE** *(over)*
> *Adorned in masters' loving art she lies . . .*

Flashes of Da Vinci, Botticelli . . .

Langdon peers down through plunging glass. On the chamber floor, far below, the smaller upright pyramid.

> **SAUNIERE'S VOICE** *(over)*
> *The blade and chalice guarding o'er Her gates . . .*

Langdon looks up at the myriad of lights.

> **SAUNIERE'S VOICE** *(over)*
> *She rests at last beneath starry skies.*

As he goes down on his knees, CAMERA DROPS through glass, and empty space, through the tiny pyramid below, revealed as the tip of a giant pyramid-shaped cavern.

A SINGLE SARCOPHAGUS. Mary's final resting place. Settle on a finely etched face staring upward. Familiar. Sophie's face.

FINAL FADE TO BLACK

Afterword

BY JOHN CALLEY

id you get that book?"

It's an innocent question, but certainly one I'll always remember with pleasure. It was the summer of 2003 and I was spending some restful time at my home in Canada when the phone rang. In those days I was chairman of Sony Pictures. On the line was my boss, Howard Stringer, chairman of Sony Corporation.

"I'm reading something I think you'll love," Howard said. "You've got to pick up a copy to enjoy while you're away." That was a Saturday. By Sunday evening I had bought and read Dan Brown's sensational novel *The Da Vinci Code*, and I was absolutely enthralled.

When Howard and I next spoke, he asked, "Did you get that book?" "Yes," I replied. "I bought it."

"Terrific—did you like it?"

"No . . . I mean I *bought* it—to make the movie."

That was nearly three years ago, and so much has happened since. This extraordinary thriller has gone on to sell more copies than any novel in history. Most important from a film perspective, the adaptation has been buoyed by an absolute creative dream-team. Director Ron Howard, producer Brian Grazer, and screenwriter Akiva Goldsman—men who have won Academy Awards together—have taken this novel and brilliantly guided it through the complex terrain of movie making. The care and attention to detail they have lavished upon Dan Brown's original is obvious, from every angle. It's hard to imagine a finer group to steer this ship.

The Da Vinci Code is an entertainment phenomenon unto itself, and being involved in its transformation to the screen has been nothing shy of exhilarating. But when all is said and done, I believe my feeling is the same as that of any other fan of *The Da Vinci Code* . . .

I'm glad I got that book. ∎

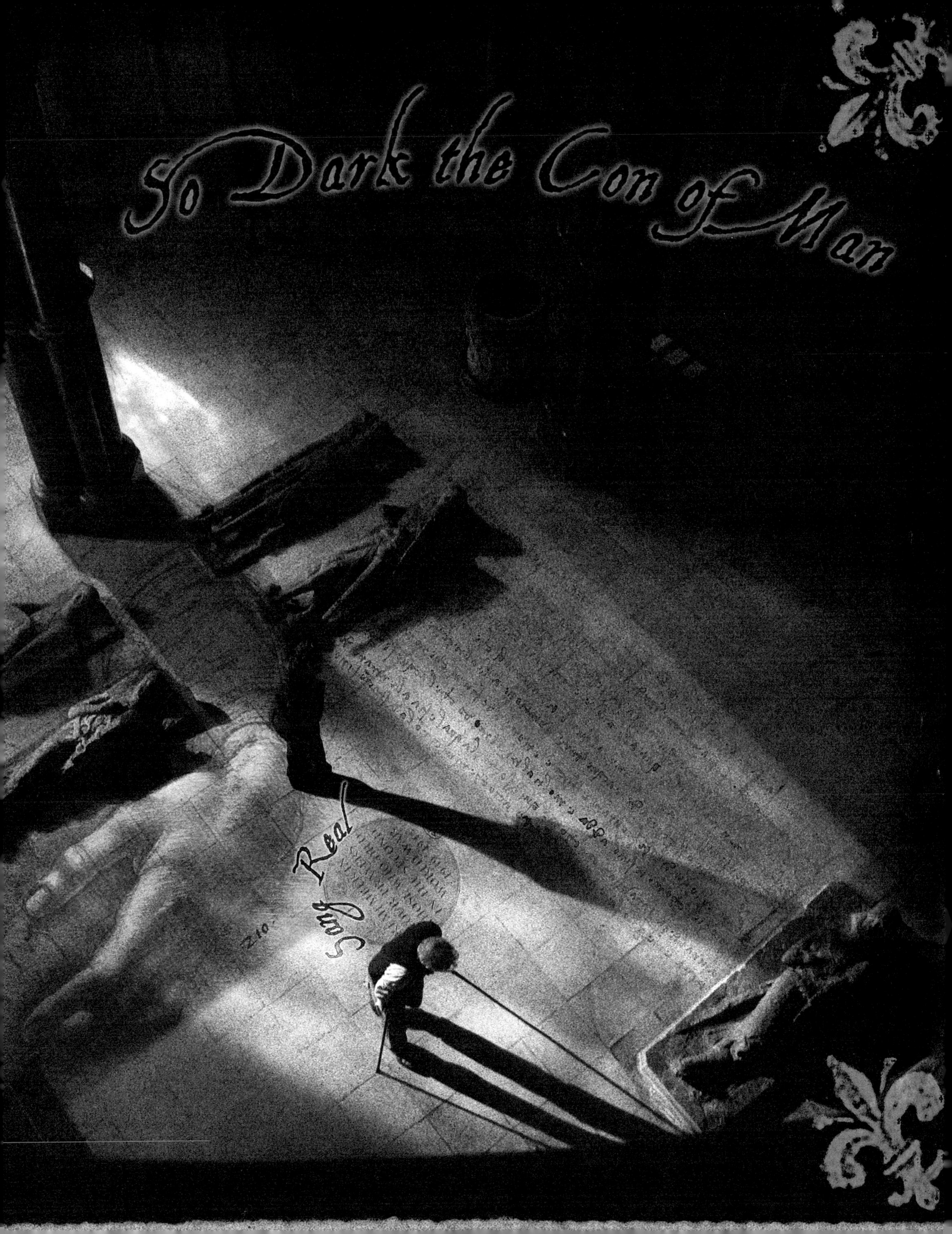
So Dark the Con of Man
Sang Real

ACKNOWLEDGMENTS

Thanks to Jason Kaufman, Editor Supreme of all things *Da Vinci* and the steady engine of this book; Consiglieri Michael Rosenberg, at Imagine; Michael Lynton, still a friend to authors everywhere; Risa Gertner and Richard Lovett at CAA; Steve Warren, Esq.; Sam Engelen, Talley Singer, and Margaret Whitman, angels who never tired; Mira, Zizzy, and Tev, as usual; and most of all to Anna Culp at Imagine, without whose dedication, obsessive attention to detail, and foolhardy optimism this book would simply not exist.

—A.G.

The game is just beginning . . . www.thedavincicodegame.com